Contents

Special Issue: Ethics Across Professions

Subscriber Information

Journal of Mass Media Ethics (ISSN 0890–0523) is published quarterly by Lawrence Erlbaum Associates, Inc., 10 Industrial Avenue, Mahwah, NJ 07430–2262. Subscriptions for Volume 19, 2004, are available only on a calendar-year basis.

Individual rates: **Print *Plus* Online:** $40.00 in US/Canada, $70.00 outside US/Canada. Institutional rates: **Print-Only:** $340.00 in US/Canada, $370.00 outside US/Canada. **Online-Only:** $320.00 in US/Canada and outside US/Canada. **Print *Plus* Online:** $375.00 in US/Canada, $405.00 outside US/Canada. Visit LEA's Web site at http://www. erlbaum.com to view free sample.

Order subscriptions through the Journal Subscription Department, Lawrence Erlbaum Associates, Inc., 10 Industrial Avenue, Mahwah, NJ 07430–2262.

Change of Address: Send change-of-address notice to Journal Subscription Department, Lawrence Erlbaum Associates, Inc., 10 Industrial Avenue, Mahwah, NJ 07430–2262.

Claims for missing issues cannot be honored beyond 4 months after mailing date. Duplicate copies cannot be sent to replace issues not delivered due to failure to notify publisher of change of address.

Journal of Mass Media Ethics is abstracted or indexed in *Communication Abstracts; Communication Institute for Online Scholarships; Columbia Journalism Review; ComIndex; Media and Values; Nordicom Finland; Public Affairs Information Service; Com Abstracts; Humanities Index; Humanities Abstracts;* EBSCO*host* Products.

Microform copies of this journal are available through ProQuest Information and Learning, P.O. Box 1346, Ann Arbor, MI 48106–1346. For more information, call 1–800–521–0600, ext. 2888.

Requests for permission should be sent to the Permissions Department, Lawrence Erlbaum Associates, Inc., 10 Industrial Avenue, Mahwah, NJ 07430–2262.

For more information, including a comprehensive index, see www.jmme.org.

Journal of Mass Media Ethics, *19*(3&4), 157–160
Copyright © 2004, Lawrence Erlbaum Associates, Inc.

Foreword

In the mid-1970s, a fledgling American industry in media ethics publications was hatched, and serious discussions about moral principles applied to the media struggled to life in the wake of the Watergate investigations. It marked the first significant discussions that cautioned against blind acceptance of the dogma and conventions of various media industries, and certainly the first sustained ethics scholarship since the dogma oriented literature of the early 1930s.

The central focus of this new endeavor was to understand how media practitioners could—and should—base ethics decisions on a variety of defensible elements, with historic practices and conventions only a part of the moral mix. In the ensuing decades, media ethicists have been looking warily over their shoulders at their fellows from other professional areas, most of whom have far more longevity than do the media folks. At the *Journal of Mass Media Ethics*, at least, we have wondered how the fledgling media work compares with that of others in the broad professional ethics arena.

The 2003 incarnation of the Colloquia 2000 series on Applied Media Ethics—the fourth in a decade-long series—offered an opportunity for application of various comparative yardsticks testing media ethics maturity. A colloquium and conference titled "Ethics Across the Professions" at the University of South Florida St. Petersburg was highlighted by the work of 15 ethicists. Host Jay Black selected five three-scholar teams, with one member of each team being an ethics specialist in a nonmedia profession. This assured the colloquium and conference of integrating voices from fields such as medical, business, engineering, legal, environmental, and general professional ethics. Each team produced a topic and a paper, as this theme issue of JMME demonstrates. The teams' work reflected concerns of interest to most areas of professional ethics and concerns of particular interest to media ethicists: the nature of accountability, obligation, power, virtue, and professional–client relationships.

Perhaps of more immediate interest, the nonmedia ethicists were invited to draft a Report Card after absorbing media ethics literature and observing media ethicists at work. In particular, they were asked to hold a general professional ethics yardstick up to that media ethics work and comment on what they found.

Four ethicists responded. Their Report Cards lead this special issue on Ethics Across Professions. Generally, they gave good marks, but pointed to weaknesses that will be instructive to those in the field.

Beyond the Report Cards, this issue of JMME contains an interesting and eclectic group of articles, the collegial product of dissimilar backgrounds.

The first article, by Lisa Newton, Lou Hodges, and Susan Keith, establishes a set of rough yardsticks about professional accountability and responsibility. The authors do not quite agree among themselves: Newton sees similarities in accountability and responsibility, however Hodges (particularly considering journalism) sees responsibility defining proper conduct and accountability compelling it. In journalism, of course, the question is one of achieving accountability. Keith provides a discussion of accountability mechanisms, noting that some are invisible and informal. She recommends that journalists might adapt the medical community's system of morbidity and mortality conferences (open discussions with management, staff, and sometimes outside experts) or they might borrow from law enforcement's and government's Internal Affairs and ethics committee investigations.

The next two articles, the first written by Wendy Barger and Ralph Barney, the second by an engineering ethicist, Michael Davis, demonstrate one divide between media ethicists and those of other professions. Barger and Barney present their best argument for journalistic and citizen moral obligations to society, and Davis replies that the two media folks fail to use the appropriate concepts and terminology and to persuade that journalism ethics is unique among professional fields. Davis does not fault the Barger–Barney main thesis and conclusions, but wonders how they got there on the route they took. Read as a whole, the work of these three scholars demonstrates the difficulties media and the public undergo in articulating their roles in a democratic system.

The nature of power is investigated by Peggy Bowers, Christopher Meyers, and Anantha Babbili. Drawing from several fields in professional ethics, and aided by insights into global culture, the authors explore the use and misuse of power (at individual, institutional, and global levels). They note that a basic purpose of journalism is to provide information vital to enhancing citizen autonomy, but see this goal as being in direct tension with the power that news media hold and wield. Constrained by proceduralism, journalists are led to misuse power at the individual level, while unwittingly surrendering moral authority, institutionally and globally, the authors assert.

Journalism and virtue are the subjects of the next section. Stuart Adam, Stephanie Craft, and Elliot Cohen provide us with three perspectives on individual and corporate virtue. Ever mindful of the tension between the media's commercial and democratic foundations, the scholars examine how media professionals can individually and collectively embody virtue. Adam outlines a moral vision of journalistic authorship and craft. Next, Craft attempts to bridge individual and organizational concerns by examining the obligations of organizations to the individuals working within them. Finally, Cohen urges resistance to the powerful corporate logic that pervades news media, and claims that the virtue of courage is essential for individual journalists.

The fifth "package" of scholarship focuses on professional–client relationships. In an eclectic article, Renita Coleman and Thomas May argue for journalistic consideration of a broad group of "clients"—third parties such as families, children, and people who accidentally have had journalism done to them. Coleman and May ask journalists to consider a range of options open to media motivated to inform the public while minimizing harm. In keeping with the approach taken by all the colloquium fellows in this issue of *JMME*, the authors draw from other professions, in this case considering how the medical community and anthropologists handle such issues as confidentiality and disclosure.

The theme of ethics across the professions is carried out in the *Cases and Commentaries*, where five writers grapple with one of the better publicized issues in recent media ethics literature: the *Los Angeles Times'* imbroglio known as "The Staples Affair." The voices of media managers and business–management ethicists provide *JMME* readers with an unusual set of insights and show us that the Staples case may not have been the "nobrainer" conflict of interest case many have called it.

A hefty book review section wraps up this special double issue. Topics treated include advertising and consumer-citizens, advertising's erotic history, two general media ethics textbooks, global public relations, understanding "rules" in society and business, media coverage of the war in Iraq, and a collection of free speech profiles.

—**The Editors**

A Change in *JMME* Editorship

Two decades of dedication to the *Journal of Mass Media Ethics* are drawing to a close with the retirement of founding co-editor Ralph Barney. Professor emeritus of communications at Brigham Young University (BYU), Ralph has been a rock solid contributor to the literature and discussions of media ethics since the mid-1970s. After years "in the trenches" of newspapers, Ralph committed himself to bridging the practical with the theoretical in his roles as teacher, researcher, and steward. His has always been a provocative voice for individual moral autonomy, for responsible use of freedom.

After being a leader of the Association for Education in Journalism (pre-cursor to AEJMC) and the Society of Professional Journalists' ethics agendas in the early 1980s, he co-founded the *Journal of Mass Media Ethics* in 1984. With financial backing from BYU, he assured the fledgling publication enough support to sustain it in its first several years. Later, when Lawrence Erlbaum Associates assumed production and circulation chores for JMME, Ralph focused on shaping the media ethics debate through soliciting a series of theme issues and launching a decade-long series of colloquia on media ethics. The journal you are holding in your hand gives the latest evidence of his efforts to frame the agenda for media ethics scholarship.

On a personal note, after going to graduate school with Ralph in the late 1960s and working closely with him for several decades, I can only wish that every scholar could be as fortunate as I have been to have a mutually respectful, highly motivated, and collegial friend. I take the lead in claiming how much he will be missed; I know that many dozens of media ethicists, and thousands of students and media professionals, join me in wishing him a fully satisfying and well-deserved retirement.

With Ralph's departure as *JMME* co-editor, we welcome Lee Wilkins of the University of Missouri as Associate Editor and Tom Bivins of the University of Oregon as *JMME*'s Web master. Lee has been a stalwart member of the editorial board since 1984 and has done a great deal of work in helping maintain the enterprise. In March 2004 she hosted the fifth in the decade-long colloquium series on media ethics and will be editing the provocative papers emerging from that investigation into media and public policy. Tom is bringing to the journal the same talents he has used to develop and sustain several other Web sites, including that of the AEJMC's Media Ethics Division. I look forward to working closely with these two very talented individuals.

The new Web address for JMME, beginning immediately, is JMME.org.

—**Jay Black, founding co-editor**

Journal of Mass Media Ethics, *19*(3&4), 161–165
Copyright © 2004, Lawrence Erlbaum Associates, Inc.

Report Cards

Five philosophers from fields outside media ethics who served as Fellows at the University of South Florida St. Petersburg Applied Media Ethics colloquium on Ethics Across the Professions in 2003 were asked, after each had worked with two media-oriented Fellows on a presentation, to assess the state of media ethics in relation to professional ethics in their own fields and to submit a report card on the quality of discussion and thought they observed among media ethics participants in the colloquium. Here are the four responses received:

Michael Davis
Illinois Institute of Technology

In two respects, journalism is clearly doing pretty well. Speaking as someone familiar with engineering ethics, I saw two clear advantages journalism has over engineering:

1. Journalists write much more about their own ethics than engineers do. Not only does journalism have several journals dedicated to journalism ethics (to engineers' half or so), but a good number of books published each year and a number of journalists willing to discuss journalism's ethics in the popular press.
2. Journalism schools are much more likely to have a course devoted to journalism ethics—and, even in "technical journalism courses," much more likely than engineers to raise issues of professional ethics in the course of teaching the craft.

In two respects, however, journalism seems to me behind engineering:

1. Discussion of journalism ethics seems to be rather isolated. There is little attempt to see American journalism in a context large enough even to include what seem to me very similar undertakings in the United Kingdom or Canada. Yet, journalists seem to be able to work across national borders in ways resembling engineers or physicians rather than lawyers or professional soldiers. Engineers readily compare practices across national boundaries.

2. Discussion of journalism ethics seems to lack much of a literature connecting the thinking of journalists about their ethics with the thinking of other professions about theirs. I was surprised at how easy it was to surprise both media Fellows on my team with what are standard moves in engineering ethics. I did not hear anything at the conference to suggest that the two of them had missed some rich stream of theoretical work on journalism ethics.

Even my old friend Elliot Cohen didn't do any theory as part of his presentation at the conference.

I was also surprised at how dubious journalists seem to be about the "professional status" of journalism. This was, I thought, because they had accepted the sociological approach to defining "profession" rather than developing a philosophical theory of their own.

That's all I have to say. As I tell my students, there's no need to use one more word than necessary. Say what you have to say and shut up. I have. The conference was a pleasure.

Christopher Meyers
University of California-Bakersfield

Thank you, Ralph and Jay, for the opportunity to comment on "the state of media ethics." This is almost a truism, but, as with any subdiscipline, there is some powerful, impressive, and intellectually and philosophically sophisticated work being done. There is also some drivel.

The first problem I notice is one also present in most other areas of practical ethics: a gap between work written primarily about the purpose and ethics of news media and that written primarily for practitioners (or budding ones). The former, meta-analyses, generally employ advanced theoretical and conceptual tools; the latter too often come across as superficial how-to guides.

The work I find most impressive is that which attempts to do both; that is, it undertakes the difficult conceptual analysis of key terms like *harm, privacy, rights, public good*, and *autonomy*, and places these within a rich understanding of the practices and motivations of media organizations. This work also reveals an appreciation for moral theory. I say appreciation because, although I do not believe moral theory should be used as a kind of cookbook for solving moral dilemmas, it does facilitate a fuller discernment of the nuances present in specific problems.

Work that shows conceptual or theoretical sophistication, let alone both, clearly stands out in practical ethics literature and, unfortunately, I would say too little of it is available in journalism ethics, especially in textbooks and trade publications. Indeed, I find it indicative of the field that one of the very best books, one that shows precisely such sophistication—Edmund Lambeth's *Committed Journalism*—is now out of print; that is, it was not enough appreciated by those who teach journalism ethics to have motivated sufficient sales.

This also points to a second, related, concern: the overreliance on quantitative research. There is undoubtedly real value in knowing what people—practitioners and educators—do and think; practical ethics has to be grounded in facts. But too much quantitative work at least borders on committing the "is–ought fallacy." In pointing to such facts, authors sometimes expect readers to reach implied moral conclusions, or worse, the authors directly suggest those conclusions. That someone behaves or thinks in particular ways, however, is no evidence of whether they should. For that conclusion, one must engage in the sorts of conceptual and theoretical analyses previously noted. Furthermore, quantitative surveys give only a partial picture of reality, because there is often a profound gap between what people report they do and how they, in fact, act. Thus I would also like to see more qualitative, and fewer quantitative, studies of journalism practice showing up in the ethics literature.

As I've already noted, these gaps are also present in the ethics literature in other areas. For example, some of the texts for business ethics courses, especially those that use a Business and Society approach, are truly awful. Similarly bad are the legal ethics texts which simply promulgate the Model Rules (the American Bar Association's code of ethics) with a few case studies thrown in. By contrast, most of the literature in bioethics is much more solid. I am not sure why the latter work is so much better, but I would guess it is because of a different historical pedigree.

So where does media ethics fall in comparison to these other fields? In the lower half, but with great potential. Media, or at least journalism, organizations are more self-reflective, more self-evaluating than most. And, as our colloquium revealed, there are wonderfully bright, inquisitive, well-educated people in the field. This combination is already resulting in increasingly sophisticated work, and I very much look forward to what emerges over the coming years.

Lisa H. Newton
Fairfield University

When I was asked to evaluate the state of Communication Ethics, Lou Hodges opined that it had a long way to go to catch up to Bioethics or Business Ethics. I think he's wrong. As Aristotle pointed out, any discipline is in good shape as long as it is appropriate to its subject matter, and bioethics, business ethics, and communication ethics are three different subjects. Bioethics has as its audience mostly doctors, mostly liberally educated, and it tends toward greater philosophical sophistication. But Business Ethics is almost as surely chained to the Bottom Line as any Fortune 500 CEO. Not only is it less philosophical, but it has to be—there is no point in speculating about the metaphysical depths of business, because there aren't any. Go deep, and you find you're in some other field of social philosophy. Ethics of Communication has some amazing philosophical possibilities, most of which I have not explored, but Journalism Ethics seems to be located just where it should be—on a clear moral plane, where judgments can be formed and made, but not wafting off into the stratosphere leaving its good working newsmen way behind. There is tons of good work to be done, but there's a lot done already.

Elliot D. Cohen
Indian River Community College

There are two marks of credible applied philosophy: (a) careful development of philosophical analysis and application of philosophical theory, and (b) careful articulation of the empirical climate of the issue in question, including applicable laws, codes, and policies. In Kantian terms, "concepts without percepts are empty; percepts without concepts are blind" (*Critique of Pure Reasons*, 1781).

As a species of applied philosophy, journalism ethics inhabits this double-edged universe. In the recent conference at the University of South Florida-St. Petersburg, there appeared to me to be a "meeting of the minds" between both journalists and philosophers, a communion that attempted to meld together the best of both possible worlds. Of course, what's true of the part is not necessarily true of the whole, but in this case, I think the interactive product was both practically and philosophically enlightening.

I had the honor of working with Stuart Adam and Stephanie Craft, two journalists with a solid ability to think philosophically. Stuart Adam made an important conceptual distinction between media as the delivery system of journalism and journalism itself as a form of craft. The idea here was to locate the virtues of journalistic ethics within the practice of journalism without blending distinct ethical issues that might arise at the media level. On the other hand, Stephanie's charge was to examine the ethical status of media: Can the corporate climate of current media ownership provide a moral edifice for journalism ethics? In popular philosophical jargon, "Can a corporation be a moral person?"

My criticism of both Stuart and Stephanie was that, in their zeal to construct a philosophical edifice for their work, they tended to overlook some brute facts about the current corporate climate of journalistic practice. In focusing on journalism as a craft apart from its corporate media framework, Stuart tended to overlook the problem of how cultivation of the journalistic virtues he discussed could be thwarted by media constraints; in particular, the tendency of corporate media to fashion the news according to what conduces to its bottom line. Similarly, in looking for a moral high ground for corporate ownership of media, Stephanie tended to overlook the fact that the essential purpose of a corporation is, indeed, to maximize its bottom line.

Paradoxically, in my discussion, I found myself emphasizing relevant empirical realities of journalistic practice to provide greater balance to the philosophical insights offered by my journalism associates. What was paradoxical here is that I expected our roles would be reversed; that I would need to emphasize the philosophical dimension leaving much of the empirical work to the others. The case seemed to be much the opposite, however.

In the end, I think our association and blending produced a set of ideas that provided the relevant antagonisms between the "is" and the "ought" of journalism and media, and which tended to fulfill the two aforementioned standards of applied philosophy. Curiously, it was done, to a considerable extent, by a reversal of roles!

Journal of Mass Media Ethics, *19*(3&4), 166–190

Accountability in the Professions: Accountability in Journalism

Lisa H. Newton
Fairfield University

Louis Hodges
Washington and Lee University

Susan Keith
Rutgers University

❏ *Accountability is viewed as a civilizing element in society, with professional accountability formalized in most cases as duties dating to the Greeks and Socrates; journalists must find their own way, without formal professional or government regulation or licensing. Three scholars look at the process in a line from the formal professional discipline to suggesting problems the journalism fraternity faces without regulation to suggesting serious internal ethics conferences as 1 solution to the problem.*

Professional Accountability:
An Introduction
Lisa Newton

Accountability means no more than answerability. I answer to my superiors; whatever I do, they have a right to ask, "What are you doing (and why)," and I have a duty to give an answer, or in older language, an account. I'm told there's a police record from the 18th century, somewhere in New England, of one of my ancestors, arrested for, and I quote, "failure to give an account." Meaning what? That the constable of the watch asked him, "Why are you out so late?" and he was unwilling (or, given the dipsomaniac history of my family, unable) to give an answer that satisfied the constable of the watch. Ordinary humans, citizens, can be "called to account," asked to explain themselves; of the Lord, however, it is said that "none can stay his hand, or ask, 'what dost thou?'" The Lord, being powerful, is not accountable to anyone.

Accountability, then, is an aspect of hierarchy. Those with the power can demand that those over whom the power is held give an account, explain, or justify themselves and their acts—in order, and this seems to be implicit in the notion, that the superior may direct the accountable one to proceed with, modify, or cease action, which the superior has the right to demand, and having demanded, the inferior has the duty to obey. Also implicit is the threat, that if the account is insufficient, the accountable one will suffer consequences. Note that the definition is neutral on direction. The servant, or the appointed official, is responsible up, to the master or the one who appointed him. The elected official is responsible down, to the voters who elected him. Professionals are answerable every which way, and that is the heart of the problem of professional accountability and simultaneously half the secret of professional freedom.

To understand the forms and limits of professional accountability, in particular the accountability of journalists, we will need a quick conceptual derivation of the term. We may begin by putting accountability in one of its traditional conceptual frameworks, that of its cognate responsibility. The notion of responsibility dates back to Plato, who discusses it (in its usual translation, "cause,") in the *Phaedo*. What causes, what is responsible for, Socrates' presence in jail, when, the previous dialogue (*Crito*) has informed us, he could very well have escaped to the Phaeacians and lived comfortably for the rest of his life? That responsibility is very much in dispute (Plato, trans. 1993). According to Anaxagoras, Socrates tells us, his sitting there in jail has everything to do with the way his muscles and bones are arrayed and in general the necessities of his body, also (implied) the physical acts that brought that body into that location. According to Socrates, his sitting there has to do with the kind of person he is, and with the fact that he has decided, all things considered, that it is better to remain there than to depart for Phaeacia.

---

*Socrates' sitting in jail … has to
do with the kind of person he is.*

What were the Greeks, Anaxagoras and Socrates in this case, quarreling about? About nothing less than the ordering of the universe and about what parts were independent and primary, and what parts were dependent, secondary, and accountable (as it were) to the first. In this very early investigation of causality, they were not far from the original Hesiodic accounts of the world, in which the deliberate actions of the gods (in the context of free choices and social hierarchies) were not distinguished from the ordinary agencies of natural forces.

Current usage recognizes at least six notions of "responsibility," the multiplication coming from several fragmentations of meaning. First, we have separated out physical causation from human agency, nonexclusively—so when the sprinkler system goes off in the middle of the night on the third floor of the office building, we can agree that the presence of cleaning fluid in the heat sensor triggered the sprinkler control without excluding human agency. If we call the fluid's role "causal responsibility," we can then go down the line of human responsibility: Adam is the hapless rookie on the night cleaning squad who sprayed the cleaner into the heat sensor (he did it), Bob was the supervisor for the third floor (it was his job to make sure that nothing went wrong with the cleaning on the third floor), Bob was accountable to Clarence, the building manager who had hired Bob and Adam and was supervisor of the whole task. Clarence will probably be held culpable or to blame for the mishap, because it happened on his watch, but he might well blame Donald, who installed the heat sensors and failed to warn about their vulnerabilities, thereby failing to exercise due care and acting negligently. Or so, at least, Empire Properties, the owners of the building, will claim, when the renters of office space on the third floor sue them, or attempt to hold them liable, for the damage their offices have suffered as a result of the deluge.

Accountability in the Professions

The professional's responsibilities, and therefore the dimensions of the professional's accountability, reconstellate that hierarchy. The professional has some skill, knowledge, and ability above that of the ordinary person, or else what would he or she have to profess? The knowledge a professional has is sometimes called "esoteric," although I can think of professions where that term is bizarre; whether acquired from experience or extended study, the knowledge is there and is valuable. That knowledge is the other half of professional freedom, or *professional autonomy*—if the layman cannot understand what the professional is doing, he cannot exercise oversight over the professional. The professional ordinarily has a clientele, a category of persons who directly or indirectly profit from that expertise, and who directly or indirectly pay the professional for making it available. On both counts—to beneficiaries, as judges of the extent of the benefit, and to paying customers, in return for their gold—the professional is accountable to the clients. There was a time when doctors and lawyers at least assumed they were accountable to no one else. Duty to clients rarely exhausts the dimensions of professional accountability today, but it remains. Before the beneficiaries of professional practice, there are the certifiers— the authorities who certify the professional, issue the license, attest to the competence, and sign the papers for hiring. That judgment of competence provides two more demands for accountability. First, in issuing a license (say, to practice medicine) the state implies the right to take it back for cause; the physician is therefore accountable to the state, with the periodic obligation to show that the conditions that had to be met for the license still obtain and that the conditions for revoking it do not.

Second, for an employed professional, like an engineer or teacher, the hirer, or employer, may be the only funnel through which the clients' fees get to him; answerability is partly or completely transferred, then, from the clients to the employer. How completely or partly? If my employer tells me to treat my students in some way that is disadvantageous to them, does my duty lie to them or to the employer? When the HMO will not pay for a treatment the physician thinks necessary, and warns the physician not to mention it to the patient, the physician is in a bind that his fathers in his profession could never have dreamed.

*Does my duty lie to students
or to employer?*

What happens when my employer and my clients decide to take bit in teeth and arrange matters for their own advantage, society be damned? My university, for instance, seems to be headed that way now. It wants to reduce the course load for the students (hurrah! say the students), also reduce the teaching load for the teachers (yes!), allowing it to fire lots of adjuncts while charging the same tuition. Everyone wins! Except the society that depends on us to produce students who know certain things. Probably, given the experience of the field, the society, not to mention The New England Association of Schools and Colleges (the accrediting agency for colleges and universities in New England) and its cognates, will be not unhappy with the developments, and life will continue as usual. However, what if we keep going? Suppose, the change having been implemented, the university secretly institutes a sort of Advanced Placement program where if students will but pay the tuition for a semester's course and agree to buy the book, the student will be assigned a B– for the course, no further effort involved? (I actually had courses like that in graduate school, but let's not go there.)

Professors would be paid a half-overload fee for the course, without having to teach it; they could sign off for up to three of these courses a semester. What a great deal! Everyone's interests are furthered. Except that, of course, the students don't really know what we say they know, and eventually, we think, that's going to hurt the society. Right now, it's dishonest.

Faced with such schemes, what should the professional do? He or she should surely do something: What that expertise confers, if nothing else, is the ability to see when corners are being cut and things are going badly wrong and that people are being cheated, no matter how willingly.

Professionals have a duty to society at large, to the greater good for the greater number, whether or not their clients and their employers agree. This sort of situation spawned the somewhat odd notion of the *whistle-blower*. The whistle-blower is a subordinate, that is, someone who does not have the power to change the situation all by himself, or that's what he'd do instead of blowing the whistle; on the other hand, he seems to have the authority in some sense to determine that something is going badly wrong and that it is his responsibility to make it stop. That combination seems to apply especially to the employed professional.

---

*Professionals have a duty
to society at large … whether
… clients and employers agree.*

However, for some professionals, the picture is even more complicated. If I find myself teaching at a traditional Christian college that suddenly decides it needs to honor its inheritance in the new right-wing Christian atmosphere, and my employer and my students and the law of the state all insist that they want, really want, me to teach creationism, and I know it is not true, what is my duty now? Or if my patient wants to believe that his condition does not need surgery, and the HMO that now employs me does not want to pay for it, and the state is trying to cut medical costs, but I know that tumor has to come out soon or it will become inoperable and the patient will die from it, what do I do? There is what Hippocrates called (with respect to medicine) "the Art," and what scholars call "the Truth," that has claims beyond what any human might assert. Even if all humans on the planet decide that $2 + 2 = 5$, it is some professional's responsibility to assert that it is not. We are accountable to the truth, the right, and the just, even when humanity has abandoned them.

Responsibility, Freedom, and Trust

To whom is the professional responsible? He or she is responsible to clients, to employers, to the state (current government), to society at large beyond the state, to the Art or to Truth (and occasionally to the professional association or code that is formed to uphold it), and occasionally, when culpable of malpractice, to some reinvention of the client or class of clients through the law of torts. On the one hand, no wonder the professional is frazzled. On the other, look how free. First, in his or her responsibility to the Truth, no layman may judge. The professional has the knowledge, and only the professional can say how it should be used. Second, because the demands of all these masters cannot be met at once, and they stand against each other with the professional in the middle, no demand is sovereign. The freedom arises in the necessity of choosing, according to conscience, which of several conflicting demands will apply in any given situation. "Multiply your masters and be free."

How shall the professional be held accountable to all those masters? The traditional answer is simplicity itself: The professional shall hold himself responsible; that is part of his professional duty; and you may trust him to fulfill his duty because he is a trustworthy person. Trustworthiness has always been the defining virtue of the professional, for obvious reasons. The doctor has access to your dirtiest physical secrets, your impotence, your gonorrhea, your herpes infection. Your lawyer knows all your most questionable financial dealings; the teacher knows your weaknesses; the priest hears your confession. The usefulness of these professions to you would come to an abrupt end if you had the slightest suspicion that any of those secrets might be noised abroad, used for personal profit, or indeed given any use at all save for benefitting you. The entire weight of the beneficial professional–client relationship rests on your trust that this will not happen. The claim of professionalism, and the assurance of trustworthiness, goes on to include, beyond those previously mentioned, law enforcement officers (who are trusted with firearms), nurses, physical therapists, and psychologists. Until recently, that list included accountants, who audit the books of major corporations; more on that in the following.

Trustworthiness extends as far as the definition of "professional": We trust physicians, we don't trust used car salesmen; we trust accountants, we don't trust telemarketers; and so forth. Note that our trust is as essential to the success of the professions as is the professional's trustworthiness; if for any reason good or bad, I start distrusting my doctor and my lawyer, I essentially render them useless to me. For professions to serve us, trust must be institutionalized.

"Trustworthiness" (with its correlate "trust") is an essential but limited and individualistic answer to the question, How shall we know that our professionals are doing their job? The integrity of the individual human being is a bulwark against dishonesty and betrayal, and we have counted on it for centuries. These last decades have reminded us that in vulnerable human beings, integrity can be dissolved in a flash under the influence of a powerful and corrupt culture. Then the trustworthiness breaks down; the greedy doctor starts prescribing a multitude of pills from his own pharmacy; the greedy accountant starts signing off on dubious deals to enrich himself; trustworthiness disappears in a matter of a few years, and trust is wiped away in a minute.

What do we do when that trust is breached (which it always will be, professionals being human)? Beyond the trust there is the institutionalized distrust, the mechanisms that back up our assumption that sooner or later, trust will be betrayed. It consists in a network of overseers, and we rely on that network as our backup. This network is the second answer to the previous question. The "impaired physician," as he is called in our law; that is the physician who is drunk, insane, drug-addicted, or otherwise unable to practice, is liable to apprehension by state committees that remove him from practice. Physicians are taught, from medical school on, that they have a duty to report impaired physicians to the state committees for everyone's good—theirs, the physicians', and the public's. There are similar mechanisms for reporting, removing from practice, punishing, and rehabilitating impaired psychotherapists, lawyers, and engineers. Accountants do not have the category of "impaired": They are either honest or dishonest, and if dishonest, the oversight boards (Financial Accounting Standards Board and the like) must overrule their judgments. There is a whole safety net for the professions, a system of watchers to make sure that the licenses the state has issued are still worthy. Otherwise they will be revoked.

---

*Beyond the trust there
is the institutionalized distrust ...
[to] back up our assumption that
... trust will be betrayed.*

How do these systems to insure integrity work? The first, and most amazing, observation is that the individualistic mechanisms work extremely well. Physicians, over the vast majority of the field, do not hurt or neglect their patients, no matter what. Lawyers are faithful to their clients. Engineers, despite the conflicts, hold paramount the safety of the public. In addition, for 60 years and more, the integrity of the auditors at Arthur Andersen and the other auditing firms was sufficient to guarantee the honesty of the reports of American business to the American people.

How do the secondary mechanisms work—the institutionalizations of distrust? Not well at all. The state boards assigned to watch over physicians and lawyers are overworked, underfunded, and not very effective. When was the last time a lawyer was disbarred for unprofessional conduct? Engineers do not do much better, nor do the appointed boards to oversee the auditors seem to be able to do their jobs. In the end, the most effective secondary mechanism for enforcing integrity in the professions, once individual virtue has failed, is the law of torts. The malpractice suit, for law or medicine, the civil suits against the accounting firms after the Enron-series debacles, are the only really effective enforcement mechanism we seem to have.

Is there some way, some better way than the enrichment of greedy law-yers through a civil suit, to keep our professions honest? Is there some better way to institutionalize our right to distrust, our right to demand an account, our right to enforce professional accountability?

Accountability in Journalism
Louis Hodges

How should we define Accountability? Accountability means answer-ability, but that observation is not helpful. One who gives an accounting of his performance to anyone to whom it is owed seeks to explain what he did and why, by offering justification for his choices between what to do and what to avoid doing. To make her point, Lisa went back to Plato; I will go back to my wife, Helen. She often calls on me to give an account of myself: "You did not mow the grass today; why?" She expects me not only to ex-plain why I chose not to cut the grass but to give reasons that justify my choice, to reveal the circumstances under which any conscientious and car-ing husband would have rightly chosen not to run the mower.

My colleague, Lisa Newton, equates accountability with responsibility. Although in some sense it is appropriate, I think it is helpful to assign the two words to distinctly different things. Each term represents a sensible and con-venient label for society to attach to two distinct societal needs. The first need, in a world where specialization of labor is acute and essential, is to de-termine how to assign different areas of work and service to individuals and groups. Who will be primarily in charge of what? Whom should we desig-nate to look after health care, for instance? To whom should we assign the running of legal systems? Who ought to be responsible for matters spiritual? Who should see to the accumulation and dissemination of information and opinion people need? In short, to whom are we going to assign the several re-sponsibilities? To what will we expect journalists to respond ably?

The second societal need is to determine how we can and should moni-tor the performance of those to whom we assign responsibilities. That is what has led us to design a wide variety of mechanisms of accountability. Accountability is the word that best fits efforts to require citizens to per-form their assigned responsibilities well. Responsibility is the word that best fits our assignment of distinct areas of social concern to individuals and groups.

In journalism, then, I have found it useful to distinguish the two terms. The issue of responsibility is: To what social needs should we expect jour-nalists to respond ably? The issue of accountability is: How might society call on journalists to explain and justify the ways they perform the respon-sibilities given them? Responsibility has to do with defining proper con-duct, accountability with compelling it.

> *Responsibility has to do
> with defining proper conduct,
> accountability with compelling it.*

The distinction is clearly reflected in our common language. Notice the prepositions: we talk about being responsible for but accountable to. For example, we may be responsible for the accuracy of the information we deliver, for informing the reader about government, for not invading privacy or inflicting further hurt on victims of tragedy. However, we are accountable to a government, an editor, a court, or a reader.

The question of responsibility is logically prior to the question of accountability. We can decide what we think the press should be responsible for without looking for ways to compel press performance. We cannot, however, reasonably seek to coerce responsible press performance until we have first defined responsible performance. That is important, because we cannot reasonably demand that the press give an account of itself or improve its performance until we determine what the press is responsible for.

Whatever labels we put on these two social needs—assignment of duties on the one hand and monitoring performance on the other—it is essential that we be clear about what the two different issues are. Here's why: I think that it was confusion of responsibility with accountability that led to the press's negative, knee-jerk reaction to the so-called Social Responsibility theory of the press promoted by the Hutchins Commission in 1947. The Commission addressed press responsibility, but the working press read accountability. Journalists and news organizations did not want to be accountable to a bunch of intellectuals on the Commission who would judge their performance. The confusion may also be one of the underlying reasons the National News Council folded.

How Is Journalism Unlike Other Professions in Accountability?

Having addressed the basic matter of definition of terms, we can now turn to the issue of how the issue of accountability in journalism differs from that of other professions. (At this juncture I will hold in abeyance the question of whether journalism can meaningfully be considered a profession.) I shall mention only three differences, though I am sure there are more.

Role of the law.   In most professional occupations—including law, medicine, accounting, engineering, etc.—the ultimate instrument of professional regulation and accountability is a combination of professional societies and government agencies. That is not the case, however, in at least two professions: journalism and the clergy. The First Amendment prohibits government interference with the free press and with religion. Governments cannot impose prepublication standards and controls on the press. The First Amendment has the effect of establishing that journalism is more than mere business. Governments, however, have considerable power to call the press to account after publication. The chief instruments are the torts of libel and privacy. (We may want to look further into this relationship.) Lisa noted previously, rightly I think, that tort law is our most effective secondary mechanism.

Professional associations.   Lawyers have two basic kinds of professional associations. One is the official state Bars that establish rules to govern lawyer conduct and procedures for implementing them through official committees. These are quasi-governmental institutions, backed by the courts. The other consists of regional, state, and national voluntary associations such as the American Bar Association (ABA). Their role is largely educational and inspirational for their members.

Journalism has none of the quasi-governmental associations, and our voluntary or unofficial ones have never enjoyed the prestige and influence of the American Medical Association or of the ABA. Nevertheless, the influence of such organizations as the American Society of Newspaper Editors, Associated Press Managing Editors, Radio-Television News Directors Association, Society of Professional Journalists, and others has been helpful in persuading journalists to practice professionally. Perhaps we can look to law and medicine (and even other professions) to discover ways in which unofficial, nongovernmental associations might be more useful in journalistic accountability.

Professional schools.   All professions I know of, except journalism, rely heavily upon professional schools not only for specialized knowledge but also for the development of professionalism. The practice of medicine, for example, in the 19th century was a hodgepodge of fakery and quackery coupled with some minimal understanding of the human body. Formal education in medicine was not a requirement in a very unstructured profession. Around the turn of the century, though, medicine became thoroughly university based. It thereby benefitted from research and a growing sense of professionalism. Ties between the university and the clinic remain close. Journalism has not gone that route, and perhaps it could not and should not. Should it?

To Whom Should Journalists Be Accountable?

The formal answer is this: Basic morality dictates that individuals (or organizations) are accountable to all those whose lives and well-being are significantly affected by the professional's conduct. In our professional lives we owe an accounting to those stakeholders for whom our professional performance has significance.

> *Individuals (or organizations)*
> *are accountable to all those*
> *whose lives and well being*
> *are significantly affected*
> *by the professionals' conduct.*

The list for journalists includes at least the following: oneself, society at large, members of the audience, subjects, sources, and maybe employers and the profession of journalism. There seems to be little dispute about obligations to the audience, subjects, and sources. We do have dispute about accountability to employers, the profession, and oneself. Look at employers first.

Employers. Is the obligation to employers truly a moral one, or is it merely a contracted condition of employment? Klaidman and Beauchamp (1987) wrote:

> Although business executives of news organizations should be as concerned about profits as those who sell cars or soap, journalists should be indifferent to whether their daily work—reporting and editing—directly enhances profitability or otherwise affects an employer's interests. Otherwise journalists would regularly entangle themselves in conflicts of interest. (p. 217)

At first I found that assertion astonishing and off the wall. I cannot dismiss it, however. I think there are many parallels between a professional educator—say a philosopher—and a professional journalist. If they are to be in any meaningful way autonomous, and if they are to be distinguished from mere employees (such as hardware store clerks), their obligations surely must be primarily to the clients they serve, not primarily to the institutions in which they work. The professional journalist knows what her audience needs, and she knows how to meet those needs. The news organization simply employs her to make use of that knowledge.

My own professional circumstance in the academy may be illustrative: I have never thought that I work for Washington and Lee. I work for my students toward their enrichment. I work at Washington and Lee, an organization that also exists for its students. That dictates that my professional obligation to my clients (students) is to provide them the finest opportunity I can for their intellectual development. With Washington and Lee I have only a contractual obligation to obey certain organizational rules and to be a good citizen. I am not accountable to the University for the content of my courses in the ethics of journalism; that is my area of professional autonomy. I dare say that is what mainly distinguishes a professional occupation from a nonprofessional one.

> *So too, the journalist's primary*
> *duty ... is to her audience,*
> *not to her employer.*

So too, the journalist's primary duty qua journalist is to her audience, not to her employer. She must be accountable first and foremost to her clientele.

The profession.   Misconduct by one journalist often has the effect of damaging the reputation of the entire profession. For that reason journalists ought to hold each other accountable. The Hutchins Commission declared that "If the press is to be accountable—and it must if it is to remain free—its members must discipline one another by the only means they have available, namely, public criticism" (Leigh, 1947, p. 94). It is worth noting that only in recent years have we seen much of that. David Shaw at the *Los Angeles Times* and Howard Kurtz at *The Washington Post* are two excellent examples of professional journalists calling others to give an accounting.

Subjects and sources.   Subjects of stories are also people to whom journalists owe an account. Their lives are commonly more deeply affected by journalism than is any other constituency. That seems to make a sufficient case for accountability to them. Sources too can be severely harmed (or significantly helped) by journalistic practice.

Accountability When It Cannot Be Compelled

Because of the basic moral principle that we owe an accounting to those whom we affect, the party who affects another may well owe an accounting to the one affected even in circumstances where the affected party lacks power to compel one. It is a common occurrence in our profession that journalists can harm an audience, a subject, or a source. People in these categories often have no effective means of demanding an account of their performance, nor of seeking redress. Rape victims, for example, who are identified by the media sometimes suffer harm from their exposure, but they are often powerless to command either an accounting or reparations.

The case of *The Seattle Times* and U.S. Senator Brock Adams is an example. In 1992, just days before election day, *The Times* published accusations of sexual misconduct against Adams by eight anonymous women. Citing his inability to defend himself against unnamed accusers, Adams withdrew from the race, and he had no effective recourse against the paper.

Under other circumstances party A can be compelled to give account of itself if party B finds himself harmed, even if party A does not acknowledge a moral duty to account for its behavior. Libel suits often accomplish this accounting.

I suggest, then, that the inability of the party who is harmed to demand an account does not diminish the affirmative moral duty of the harmer to provide one. That principle should become part of the journalistic moral canon.

The existence of accountability systems opens the possibility of sanctions, which in turn encourages responsible conduct. The greater the certainty of being exposed for misconduct, the greater the likelihood of careful moral choice.

What Should Journalists Be Held Accountable For?

What should journalists be held accountable for? Should it be only for performance as journalists? Should a journalist whose professional practice is beyond reproach be sanctioned by her news organization for personal misconduct off the job? Generally, my answer is no.

Consider the recent case of Bob Greene at *The Chicago Tribune*. He was almost universally respected as an important and extraordinarily talented journalist. But he was accused of having had an affair with a teenage girl—who by the way was of the age of legal consent, but whom Greene first met during a journalistic interview (Pickett, 2002). After he was fired, some readers called to complain that Greene had betrayed their trust (Wycliff, 2002). But the predominant sentiment among those who called, so the *Tribune* reported, was in Greene's favor.

The *Tribune*'s concern shows in Editor Ann Marie Lipinski's statement that "journalists have a special obligation to avoid personal conflicts that undermine their professional standing and their trust with readers, sources, or news subjects" (Kirk & Davey, 2002). She is probably justified in that claim, because credibility is somehow at stake. But what does a journalist's sexual misconduct have to do with his competence to gather important information or opinion and pass it on to his audience? In the Greene case, no one has made that connection to my satisfaction.

The basic issue is actually quite an old one. An early manifestation appears in the Donatist controversy in 4th-century Christianity. The Donatists held that the efficacy of the sacraments was abolished if the purity of priests administering them was compromised. Under Constantine in 314 AD, however, the Church insisted that the vitality and efficacy of the sacraments lay in the sacraments themselves and not in the priests who performed them.

> *... the personal purity*
> *[of the journalist] has no effect*
> *on the quality of her journalism.*

Similarly, in the case of journalists, the personal purity of the journalist has no effect on the quality of her journalism. Good journalism must be judged by the moral standards of accuracy, importance, clarity, and so forth. It is preposterous to assert that excellent journalism can be produced only by journalists of noble character and moral purity. How many pure journalists can we name? A 64-year-old female reader of the *Tribune* put it nicely when she wondered how the paper could fire Bob Greene: "How could this happen?" she wrote. "[Is] this paper ... run by a bunch of virgins or something?" (Wycliff, 2002).

Greene's misconduct (which he admitted) with the teenager could have no significant effect on the quality of his journalism. It could, however, affect his popularity with the audience, which in turn would likely affect the *Tribune's* bottom line. In this case, it appears that more readers sided with Greene than with the editors who fired him. That fact, though, does not nullify the point that editors have every right to include nonjournalistic business decisions in matters of employment.

Private lives of journalists—such as in the Greene case—must be distinguished, however, from other kinds of conduct while not at work. We do, and should, hold them accountable for conflicts of interest. Conflicts of interest (e.g., accepting gifts from sources or subjects, holding public office, finding secondary employment with subjects) do affect the quality, accuracy, and framing of stories. That is to say, they do affect the quality of one's journalistic performance.

A Formal Standard

What, then, should the formal standard be? For purposes of our further examination of this topic, I suggest the following: "Journalists should be held accountable for their private lives only under circumstances in which their private behavior directly and seriously harms their professional performance." I reject out of hand Bob Steele's (2002) assertion that "It's a fallacy to believe that we can separate our personal and professional lives" (p. 1). I see no moral basis for journalists' employers to think they have a right to control most of the private affairs of their employees. Private life includes matters such as sex and marriage relations, religious belief and affiliation, friendships, and political philosophy or affiliation. If we come to expect reporters to be as pure as the driven snow, we will simply have no reporters.

> *"Journalists should be held accountable for their private lives only under circumstances in which their private behavior directly and seriously harms their professional performance."*

Mechanisms of Accountability
Susan Keith

Lou Hodges asserts that journalists should be held accountable for their performance as journalists (and only as journalists), and notes that accountability systems hold the prospect of sanctions, which encourage responsible conduct. That raises this question: Which accountability mechanisms most effectively encourage responsible conduct?

Although accountability mechanisms may be virtually invisible to journalism consumers, Bertrand (2000) listed more than two dozen. He, like others, divided accountability mechanisms into categories—internal, external, and cooperative—based on how they are used and by whom. Internal accountability mechanisms, used chiefly by journalists, are designed, in theory, to affect the practice of journalism from within. External mechanisms are generally employed by nonjournalists and seek to affect the practice of journalism from without. Cooperative accountability mechanisms, as the name suggests, rely on cooperation between journalists and nonjournalists, and affect or seek to affect journalism from within and without simultaneously.

It may be profitable, however, to make a further division in these commonly used categories and break internal accountability mechanisms into two groups: those narrowly targeted toward a single media outlet or media corporation and those that aim to affect the entire field of journalism from within. The former might be viewed as mechanisms that allow specific media organizations to tend to their own stoops, and the latter encourage journalists to look at the performance of their peers.

Among narrowly focused internal mechanisms generally used by journalists are as follows:

- Organizational ethics codes, such as *The New York Times'* (2003) new 53-page code or the Gannett Newspaper Division (1999) Principles of Ethical Conduct for Newsrooms.
- Published or broadcast corrections and clarifications, in which news organizations own up to their mistakes.
- Ombudsmen or reader representatives, who act as newsroom advocates for reader interests, investigating complaints, and in some cases, offering public critiques of their employers' performance.
- Internal memos, in which senior managers may set standards of behavior for their newsrooms.

The main broad-focus internal accountability mechanisms, which are generally employed by journalists with the goal of affecting behavior of their peers others, include the following:

- Codes of ethics of professional organizations, such as the Society of Professional Journalists' (SPJ, 1996) Code of Ethics or the Radio-Television News Directors Association's Code of Ethics and Professional Conduct (Radio-Television News Directors Association, 2000).
- Media coverage of the media, provided by programs like National Public Radio's "On the Media," produced by WNYC in New York; *The New York Times*, *The Los Angeles Times*, and other large newspapers; and, perhaps more important today, compilations of media-on-media reports in Web logs, or "blogs," such as Jim Romenesko's (2003) Poynter Institute hosted site, "Romenesko"; the SPJ's "Press Notes" (SPJ, 2003); or Don Fitzpatrick's broadcast-oriented "ShopTalk" (Fitzpatrick, 2003). While covering the media industry, these reports shed light on ethics-related issues. Journalists who make public missteps, for example, know they are likely to be the subject of references such as, "I read it on Romenesko."
- Coverage of the mainstream media by so-called "alternative" media, such as newspapers of the New Times chain, which often contain a column of criticism examining general interest newspapers and television news operations.

External mechanisms for accountability focus attention on journalism from outside and are generally employed by nonjournalists, including the following:

- Journalism reviews, which once were published largely by journalists, seeking to reform journalism from within (Bertrand, 1978). Today, the three surviving print journalism reviews (*American Journalism Review, Columbia Journalism Review,* and *St. Louis Journalism Review*) as well as a Web newcomer, *Online Journalism Review,* are associated with universities (Maryland, Columbia, Webster, and Southern California, respectively) and so provide external journalism critiques (Bertrand, 2000).

• Nonprofit media organizations, such as The Poynter Institute for Media Studies or the American Press Institute, whose faculty and staff comment on media performance and which provide, through Web sites and programs, forums for discussions of ethics-related issues.

• Government regulatory agencies, chiefly the Federal Communications Commission, which exerts some limited control over the content of broadcast journalism.

• Groups that assess media performance from a particular political viewpoint, such as Fairness and Accuracy in Reporting (FAIR, progressive) and Accuracy in Media (AIM, conservative).

• Projects associated with journalism schools or universities, such as Project Censored, a program of the Department of Sociology at Sonoma State University in Sonoma, California, which annually names a list of the most undercovered stories, or the Project for Excellence in Journalism at Columbia University.

• Research and commentary by individual academic scholars occasionally published in trade journals or journalism reviews.

Cooperative mechanisms for accountability depend on interactions between journalists and nonjournalists for their success. They include the following:

• News councils, such as the Minnesota News Council or the defunct National News Council, which hear complaints brought by citizens against the media and render published judgments (Bertrand, 2000). Although these might seem like purely external accountability mechanisms, they require some degree of cooperation (and perhaps funding) from news organizations if they are to be effective.

• Letters to the editors and other commentaries, written by members of the public but allowed into newspapers and onto broadcast outlets only with the cooperation and approval of journalists. These include such innovative repositories of comment as Citizen's Voice, a cross-platform feedback project of Media General convergence partners *The Tampa Tribune,* WFLA-TV, and www.tbo.com.

• How well do these accountability mechanisms work? At best, they are a mixed bag.

Among narrowly focused internal mechanisms, internal memos and corrections and clarifications may have the greatest force. A message from a senior editor or producer that a behavior is unacceptable carries at least the implied threat of demotion or firing for those who routinely engage in it. Publishing or broadcasting correction and clarification is fairly common, perhaps because it often is not only the ethical but also the pragmatic thing to do, particularly in states where retraction statutes reduce libel damages recoverable from defendants who correct errors (Pember, 2003). Journalism's dirty little secret, however, is that many errors go uncorrected because complaints are ignored, complaints never reach the right person or—worse—victims of errors feel so helpless in the face of a monolithic media organization they never call. This was brought to light after Jayson Blair was found to have concocted conversations, descriptions, and entire stories for *The New York Times*. One victim of Blair's butchery told *Columbia Journalism Review*, "When it comes to the media, I leave it alone" (Hassan, 2003, p. 19).

> *Journalism's dirty little secret is*
> *… errors that go uncorrected.*

Codes of ethics and ombudsmen also are not as effective as they might be. Although codes written for particular organizations could be enforced by management, they often are not. In addition, studies have shown that individual journalists may not buy into codes if they had little to do with their creation or if the codes, or ethics in general, are rarely discussed in their newsrooms (Boeyink 1994, 1998; Pritchard & Morgan, 1989). Use of internal critics, ombudsmen, or reader representatives has never truly caught on. Although there were 1,468 U.S. daily newspapers in 2001 (Newspaper Association of America, 2002), there were only about 40 newspaper ombudsmen or reader representatives (Hentoff, 2003).

Among the more broadly focused internal accountability mechanisms, codes of ethics of professional organization remain problematic because they are unenforceable. Major journalism organizations do not routinely kick out members who violate their ethics codes. More benefit is probably produced by coverage of media in mainstream and alternative publications. No journalist wants to be embarrassed among his or her peers, and coverage of one media outlet's foibles by another media outlet offers the opportunity for public castigation. The instructive effect of such negative publicity may be limited, however, if it comes from a so-called "alternative" publication that is viewed as less than professional in its own practices or as having its own ethics-related problems (such as earning significant revenue from advertisements for sex-industry services). Even coverage by mainstream media outlets may be dismissed if it appears to be motivated by professional jealousy.

External and cooperative mechanisms, institutionalizations of distrust, fare even worse. Recent studies have shown that the journalism reviews have little impact on the behavior of journalists because few journalists read them regularly (Fee, 2001; Keith, 2003; Weaver & Wilhoit, 1996). Research on media practices by academics is similarly doomed, because too much of it never reaches even the journalism review and trade press that most journalists aren't reading. The media may also have a tendency to dismiss such research as irrelevant Ivory Tower ramblings. News councils have never been popular, largely because of the financing and effort required to sustain them, and the buy-in from media needed for them to be effective. Concerns expressed by groups such as FAIR and AIM have such ideological baggage they are easily ignored.

That leaves three types of external or cooperative mechanisms: letters to the editor or other types of citizen commentary, which can be effective if produced in great volume; criticism voiced by or through nonprofit media organizations like the Poynter Institute, which may carry some weight with journalists because of their perceived neutrality; and government regulation, through such agencies as the FCC. Assuming that most practitioners and lovers of journalism would agree that increased government interference in journalism would not be good, we are left with only two tools for media accountability that are both effective and palatable. That hardly seems enough.

Perhaps it is time to turn
to other professions and trades
for ideas

If more than 30 years of intense focus on media ethics have not given journalism all the accountability mechanisms it needs, perhaps it is time to turn to other professions and trades for ideas. As Lisa Newton asked, are there better ways than now exist to institutionalize our right to distrust, our right to demand an account, our right to enforce professional accountability? Well, yes.

Journalism could learn at least one thing from medicine, a profession it usually regards as an unfit exemplar because of its reliance on licensure, a mechanism at odds with journalism's desire to remain free to investigate all authorities. In medicine, the worst outcome of practice—death—is investigated in weekly or monthly hospital morbidity and mortality (M&M) conferences, which one renowned teaching program describes as "a cornerstone of quality improvement." At these conferences, "open discussion among residents and faculty is intended not to find fault, but to seek better understanding of the events, to educate, and to suggest changes in management or departmental protocols to reduce the risk of future complications" (Department of Surgery, Yale University School of Medicine, 2002).

Postmortems do occasionally occur in journalism. *The Washington Post* conducted an investigation and published the results in the wake of Janet Cooke's 1981 fabrication of the Pulitzer Prize-winning story "Jimmy's World" (Green, 1981). *The Los Angeles Times* had media writer David Shaw produce a fourteen-page expose on its involvement in the Staples Center scandal of 1999 (Shaw, 1999). In summer 2003, *The New York Times* held a meeting for several hundred newsroom employees to discuss Blair's repeated plagiarism and fabrication (Perry, 2003) and printed a 13,900-word explanation of which stories were affected (Barry, Barstow, Glater, Liptak, & Steinberg, 2003).

It seems, however, that no journalism organizations regularly conduct the newsroom equivalent of M&M conferences—call them "ethics and morality" meetings—designed to assess, in a spirit of learning, when the news organization has done well and when its performance has been lacking.

The reasons are obvious. "We don't have time for another meeting," the busy editor or producer will say. Medicine, however, would suggest that there is always enough time enough to consider avoiding past mistakes. "We already do that in the morning meeting," another editor or producer will add. But a morning planning meeting, however lengthy, occurs too close to the previous day's news production cycle to allow for adequate hindsight about performance. In addition, a morning meeting is, of necessity, too dominated by planning related to dissemination of the current day's news to provide adequate opportunity for the sober reflection, questioning, and evaluation that could occur at an ethics M&M conference.

A newsroom M&M conference …
should include staff from all
levels; … have mechanisms for
anonymous comment.

A newsroom ethics M&M conference might be scheduled once a month or as rarely as twice a year. But it should include staff members from all levels—clerks to senior reporters and tape editors to news directors—just as medical M&M conferences include all members of a medical service: medical students, nurses, interns, residents, and attending physicians. Commentary should be sought from all levels, and there should be mechanisms for anonymous comment so that ideas from wise people low in the organizational hierarchy might be heard without fear of retribution. When possible, it might be worthwhile to have an outside facilitator—or at least the reader representative or ombudsman, where one existed—lead the discussion.

Clearly, there would be risks involved. It would take a brave editor or news director to encourage public discussion of the "rightness" of past decisions, which probably were made largely by the editor or news director. Arthur Sulzberger Jr., Howell Raines, and Gerald Boyd—the current publisher, former editor, and former managing editor, respectively, of *The New York Times*—could attest to this. When they met with staff members after Blair's misdeeds came to light, the response was "a mixture of anger and sorrow" (Berkowitz, 2003, p. A4).

Attorneys might fret that such discussions would become public, as what was said at the employees-only *Times* staff meeting did (Steinberg, 2003), and be used against the media outlet in litigation. It must be acknowledged, too, that there are qualitative differences between what is assessed at a M&M conference and what would be considered at a newsroom ethics conference. Death is a final, all-or-nothing condition, easily identified by a lack of vital signs. Whether an ethics misstep has even occurred might be endlessly debated. At least, however, an ethics conference might institutionalize a place for regular ethics-related discussions, which may not now occur in some newsrooms (Boeyink, 1994; Keith, 2003).

Journalism also might learn from the ways police and state governments police themselves. Most large law enforcement organizations have an Internal Affairs Division that investigates suspected wrongdoing by those who are charged with apprehending wrongdoers. Many state governments have ethics committees that consider violations of ethics policies by those ostensibly committed to public service and sometimes offer advisory opinions before questionable action is taken. Although neither body may be a favorite of those whose actions it considers (and Internal Affairs Divisions are themselves subject to corruption), both have the potential to serve useful functions in protecting the public from rogue professionals.

Such formal policing committees probably would not work in journalism. Journalists often are wary of authority, including that of their bosses. In addition, in a field dominated by corporate ownership that is perhaps overly responsive to market considerations, formal ethics disciplinary committees could be seen as, or turn into, mechanisms for staff reduction. That does not mean, however, that news organizations should not have a formal mechanism for considering ethical conduct of their employees. Most midsize to large newsrooms have some sort of annual performance review that assesses such issues as productivity and adherence to dead-

line. Could not adherence to ethics standards be made a part of such evalu-
ations? Giving ethics as much attention during the annual performance review as making deadline or producing stories, pages, or packages would
at least send the message that ethics was important.

---

*Journalism could also learn
from the education and training
requirements in a host
of professions.*

Journalism could also learn from the education and training requirements in a host of professions, including medicine, architecture, and ele-
mentary and secondary education. Architects, teachers, and many types of
medical professionals must take part in continuing education to retain
their place in their professions. Although this continuing education is
rarely, if ever, ethics-related, it does help professionals serve their clients
better by allowing them to remain up to date in their specialized body of
knowledge. Because journalists are not certified or licensed, they have no
such requirements. In fact, so many get little or no postbaccalaureate training that a lack of training was the found to be the number one reason for job
dissatisfaction in a survey commissioned by the Council of Presidents of
National Journalism Organizations (Truitt, 2002). More important, significant numbers of journalists begin their jobs with no training whatsoever in
ethical decision-making, because their university programs required no
courses in philosophical or applied ethics (Keith, 2003).

Journalism organizations could improve their accountability, and perhaps their credibility with sources and news consumers, with a real commitment to ongoing ethics training. Such training would need to go beyond repackaging information found in the organization's code of ethics,
and instead focus on how to make decisions in situations not covered by
the code. It should be offered not only to front-line reporters and editors,
who are likely to make low-level ethics-related decisions, but also to senior
managers, whose macrolevel decisions will set the tone for how ethical a
news outlet is.

These proposed accountability mechanisms are not without problems.
Who is to conduct the ethics M&M meeting? If it is a senior manager, can
the exercise ever be anything more than a reinforcement of the status quo?
If ethics becomes a component of the annual evaluation, whose ethics are
used? What is the scale? If ethics-related training is offered to journalists,
who will provide it? And when? More important, each of the "borrowed"
accountability mechanisms offered here is internal. None provides a satis-

factory answer to the question "Are there better ways than now exist to institutionalize our right to distrust, our right to demand an account, our right to enforce professional accountability?"

There are, however, ways that groups external to, but interested in, journalism could seek an accounting. First, citizens could create forums for discussion of journalistic behavior and use the light of publicity to force an accounting. In many U.S. cities, cable access television provides an outlet for resident-produced programming. Citizens interested in media performance could start their own programs evaluating the performance of media, perhaps with guidance from interested journalism professors. They might also post the results of their monitoring of local media performance on Web sites, creating electronic, citizen-produced versions of the paper and reporter-produced journalism reviews that proliferated in the 1970s (Bertrand, 1978). The largest stumbling block to such efforts, of course, is that they would need strong leaders who could accurately identify excellence and evil in journalism, rather than merely grind political axes. In addition, to make a lasting difference, leaders of such efforts would have to make long term commitments, something many of the journalists who published local journalism reviews in the 1970s ultimately could not.

Scholars of journalism ethics
might take training in ethical
decision making directly
to journalists.

In addition, scholars of journalism ethics might take training in ethical decision-making directly to journalists, as some have in the past (Hernandez & Schmitt, 1996) and as ethics experts in other fields do ("NSF Funds Chapter-Based Ethics Workshhops," 2001). A good model exists in the "Quick Courses" conducted in several cities yearly by the Society for News Design, an industry group for newspaper, magazine, and online designers. That group typically rounds up trainers and flies them to midsize to large cities, where they conduct six to eight hours of training during a single day, frequently in a newspaper's meeting room or auditorium. Professionals from the host publication and others in the region pay a nominal fee to attend. Ethics decision-making training conducted on such a model would need the imprimatur of a journalism organization, like the American Press Institute, a journalism foundation, a university, or some other institution that journalists would regard as politically neutral. It could, however, feature as panelists members of organizations with a variety of reasons for demanding an account from journalists. The trick, of course, would be getting news organizations to support such training and finding pedagogical strategies to make the training memorable after the workshop had ended.

At the end of the day, solving the media accountability puzzle may not be so much a case of finding the perfect accountability mechanism, as one of creating a patchwork of mechanisms. If journalists are continuously held accountable on multiple levels (internally and externally) by multiple parties (bosses, peers, clients, and themselves), we may come closer to a journalism that adequately serves society.

References

Barry, D., Barstow, D., Glater, J., Liptak, A., & Steinberg, J. (2003, May 11). Correcting the record: Times reporter who resigned leaves long trail of deception. *The New York Times*, late edition, p. A1.

Berkowitz, H. (2003, May 15). Times tries to restore faith, calm staff anger. *Newsday*, Nassau and Suffolk edition, p. A4.

Bertrand, C.-J. (1978, September). *A look at journalism reviews, Freedom of Information Center Report 19*. Columbia: University of Missouri.

Bertrand, C.-J. (2000). *Media ethics and accountability systems*. New Brunswick, NJ: Transaction.

Boeyink, D. (1994). How effective are codes of ethics? A look at three newsrooms. *Journalism Quarterly, 71*, 893–904.

Boeyink, D. (1998). Codes and culture at the Courier-Journal: Complexity in ethical decision making. *Journal of Mass Media Ethics, 13*, 165–182.

Department of Surgery, Yale School of Medicine. (2002). *Surgical education*. New Haven, CT: Department of Surgery, Yale School of Medicine. Retrieved July 23, 2003, from http://yalesurgery.med.yale.edu/surgeryeduc/conf.html

Fee, F., Jr. (2001, March). *Connecting with the news culture: Trade-press readership among copy editors and their supervisors*. Paper presented at the 26th annual Association for Education in Journalism and Mass Communication Southeast Colloquium, Columbia, South Carolina.

Fitzpatrick, D. (2003). *Shop talk*. New York: Vault.

Gannett Newspaper Division. (1999). *Gannett Newspaper Division principles of ethical conduct for newsrooms*. McLean, VA: Author. Retrieved July 23, 2003, from http://www.asne.org/ideas/codes/gannettcompany.htm

Green, B. (1981, April 19). Janet's world. *The Washington Post*, p. 1.

Hassan, A. (2003, July/August). Blair's victims: That helpless feeling. *Columbia Journalism Review*, p. 19.

Hentoff, N. (2003, July 21). Post-Blair, newspapers need ombudsmen. *Editor & Publisher*. Retrieved July 23, 2003, from http://www.mediainfo.com/editorandpublisher/featurescolumns/articledisplay.jsp?vnucontentid=1938296

Hernandez, D., & Schmitt, B. (1996, October 19). SPJ approves ethics code. *Editor & Publisher*, pp. 22–23.

Keith, S. (2003). *Ethics and newspapers' final gatekeepers: Work conditions and copy editors' role conceptions.* Unpublished doctoral dissertation, University of North Carolina at Chapel Hill.

Kirk, J., & Davey, M. (2002, September 16). Breech of trust ends Greene's career at Tribune. *The Chicago Tribune.* Retrieved July 30, 2003, from http://www.chicagotribune.com/news/chi-0209160216sep16.story

Klaidman, S., & Beauchamp, T. (1987). *The virtuous journalist.* New York: Oxford University Press.

Leigh, R. (Ed.). (1947). *A free and responsible press.* Chicago: University of Chicago Press.

The New York Times. (2003). *Ethical journalism.* New York: Author

Newspaper Association of America. (2002). Number of U.S. daily newspapers. In *Facts about newspapers 2002.* Retrieved July 23, 2003, from http://www.naa.org/info/facts02/12facts2002.html

NSF funds chapter-based ethics workshops. (2001). *American Scientist, 89*(3), 285.

Pember, D. (2003). *Mass media law* (2003–2004 ed.). Boston: McGraw-Hill.

Perry, J. (2003, May 26). Sign of the times. *U.S. News & World Report,* p. 46.

Pickett, D. (2002, September 19). Tribune columnist Bob Greene fired over 'inappropriate sexual conduct.' *The Chicago Tribune,* news special edition, p. 4.

Plato. (1993). *The last days of Socrates* (H. Tredennick, Trans.). London: Penguin.

Pritchard, D., & Morgan, M. (1989). Impact of ethics codes on judgments by journalists: A natural experiment. *Journalism Quarterly, 66,* 934–941.

Radio and Television News Directors Association. (2000). *Code of ethics and professional conduct.* Retrieved July 30, 2003, from http://www.rtnda.org/ethics/coe.shtml

Romenesko, J. (2003). *Romensko.* Retrieved July 23, 2003, from http://www.poynter.org/column.asp?id=45

Shaw, D. (1999, December 20). Crossing the line—Behind the Staples affair. *The Los Angeles Times,* pp. V1–14.

Society of Professional Journalists. (1996). *Code of ethics.* Indianapolis, IN: Society of Professional Journalists. Retrieved July 30, 2003, from http://www.spj.org/ethicscode.asp

Society of Professional Journalists. (2003). *Press notes.* Retrieved July 23, 2003, from http://www.spj.org/pressNotes.asp?ref=4195

Steele, B. (2002, September 19). *The personal is professional: Lessons learned from Bob Greene's demise.* Retrieved October 2, 2002, from http://www.poynter.org

Steinberg, J. (2003, May 15). Editor of *Times* tells staff he accepts blame for fraud. *The New York Times,* late edition final, p. A31.

Truitt, R. (2002, June). Journalists decry lack of training. *Presstime,* p. 20.

Weaver, D., & Wilhoit, G. (1986). *The American journalist.* Bloomington: Indiana University Press.

Wycliff, D. (2002, September 19). A trust bestowed, a trust betrayed. *The Chicago Tribune,* p. 25.

Journal of Mass Media Ethics, *19*(3&4), 191–206

Media–Citizen Reciprocity as a Moral Mandate

Wendy Barger
University of St. Thomas

Ralph D. Barney
Brigham Young University

❏ *A participatory democracy necessarily minimizes legal restraints on its citizens, substituting, for the common good, moral obligations to contribute with their activities. This article argues that a democratic society is endangered unless both media and citizens accept reciprocal moral obligations related to the distribution and use of information. Journalists are expected to facilitate distribution of information and engage citizens usefully in the knowledge process, fueling the participatory engine that drives a democracy. Citizens, in return, have a reciprocal obligation to expose themselves to useful information, respond publicly, tolerate (and even encourage) diversity, and protect media autonomy.*

This article is essentially an essay on power, its accumulation and its use. It also explores the constant power struggles characteristic of a competitive society. The article is particularly concerned with moral obligations of journalists and citizens to refuse to allow themselves to be victimized by power brokers, to assert enough control over their own actions that they knit, rather than rip, the fabric of a healthy democratic society.

Central to such power struggles are the mass media that can either (a) serve as a bastion to enable citizens, through timely access to information, to accumulate the power necessary to somewhat avoid being victimized and to control their own destinies, or (b) socialize citizens into a general conformity in which autonomy is largely lost. In the former situation, media and citizens must accept a moral obligation to maintain a climate in which great quantities of information may flow without regulations, conventions, and restrictions that are the hallmark of traditional cultures.

This article concentrates on the role of media in the former case, and argues of an obligation of individual citizens to carry their share of the democratic burden.

To recognize the stark differences, it must be explained that, generally, the world can be divided into two very different types of cultural systems.

In one system, with highly predictable commonalties, traditional hierarchies automatically bestow power. Thus, lifetime roles are determined by circumstances of birth and family affiliation. Questions of power and behavior are predetermined by decisions made generations earlier that sought to eliminate divisive influences of power seeking. This, of course, is comforting in that it relieves community members of the stress of having to fight for their own niche. Very simply, the primary moral responsibility of a citizen in traditional communities is to follow rules and obey authority. Among these citizens, change is resisted. They are gripped by a strongly rule-oriented (an unthinking deontological) existence that raises principle to the level of absolute, enshrining mostly communal values. Traditional cultures that do try to adapt to a modern world are often thrown into cultural and physical upheavals, pitting ancient against modern.

The second type of cultural system—like that found in the United States—allows, but does not mandate, participation and fosters the competition and power struggles that produce change and, arguably, progress. In this culture, one may be largely what one makes of oneself in often fierce and messy competition with fellow citizens. Here, rules tend be broken to create change, and discovery is largely unassigned. Nearly anyone can be a change agent or can make discoveries that affect society. These discoveries result in products of individual creativity and enterprise that meet a perceived need, often for profit. Moral obligations in this society are much greater and more varied than in a traditional culture. In contrast to the compelled morality of traditional cultures, individuals in countries such as the United States participate as they decide to, accepting moral obligations in individualistic ways.

The Idea of Democracy

The U.S. Bill of Rights created the climate for an individualistic society by obliging the government to keep citizens safe without unduly interfering in their lives. In a more mundane but profound way, citizens were given the right to act individually in their own pursuits. In terms of lifestyles—education levels, opportunities, the general health and well-being of the populace—the culture has tended to sort out its problems in the absence of central control of either politics or the economy. Key to the success of this system must be citizen participation. The expressed creativity of individuals, their contributions multiplied by nearly 300 million, creates a culture that often appears to be in chaos and mired in individualism, not to mention moral relativism. Nevertheless, such a culture has generally forged ahead in the development of new ideas and in enviable lifestyles.

Perhaps the most dramatic recent example of such individualistic contributions is the development of Bill Gates' computer software empire. A

Harvard dropout, Gates and a small group of associates shepherded the Microsoft system to its preeminent position by violating accepted conventions of truth-telling, in offering a product to IBM that did not exist. He then developed that product to fit the promise (Every, 2002). No one assigned Gates the task, but as a result of his ingenuity and drive, the ponderous MS-DOS system was developed. This led to the Windows operating system that revolutionized the operation of an already revolutionary device, the personal computer. Parenthetically, the MacIntosh operating system, with its mouse and icon-driven functions, preceded Windows, but failed in its power struggle with the Gates/Microsoft juggernaut. Although most citizens find themselves in a more routine role than the one Gates pursued, basic principles suggest a commonality.

A society's cumulative decisions determine its complexion and its progress, profoundly affecting its members. Individuals participate in society by contributing their decisions, and these contributions not only serve self-interest but, importantly, also ferret out community needs.

The Marketplace Analogy

Perhaps the most routine individual citizen participation takes place in the economic arena, where individual dollars are essentially "votes" for a product. A product or service lives or dies according to the number of votes cast for it. As the self-interest of the buyer is served by the purchase of a necessary or desired product, community interest is served by strengthening support for that product or service.

The moral question lies in the quality of the decision to cast the vote and in the quality of the product the vote purchases. It would seem unassailable that consumers have a moral obligation—both to themselves and to their community—to spend their money in ways that will be of mutual benefit and will not unjustly enrich vendors for inferior products. For this to happen, buyers should accept a moral obligation to their fellow citizens to be careful selectors of products and not allow themselves to be victimized by the bombardment of persuasive messages from product managers competing for consumer dollars. To bend to undue persuasive influences and purchase an inferior or unneeded product is to further an unjust power accumulation for a purveyor of such products. In consolidating power, the producer of inferior products is encouraged to do more of the same and to further victimize disinterested consumers through promotional resources provided by the early buyers.

Thus, a healthy consumer society is perpetuated by well-educated, knowledgeable, and thoughtful consumers who seek the best buys for their money. One might argue that citizens have a moral obligation to contribute their economic votes in thoughtful ways in reciprocation for their fellows also making thoughtful decisions that benefit them as individuals, as well as the entire society. An individualistic culture will find it difficult to survive unless a critical mass of rational people accept moral obligations to make thoughtful, informed buying decisions.

Information Consumption

So it is with the consumption of information. A utilitarian greatest-good-for-the-greatest-number perspective, consistent with Mill's (1859/1956) enhancement of life for the individual, is served by consumers who both press their media for high quality information and act on that information in responsible ways. Unfortunately, as the number and special interests of media outlets has expanded and the complexity of issues facing the individual has increased, more and more citizens seem to shrink from such a moral obligation and retreat to one of two positions.

> *As the complexity of issues increases, more citizens seem to shrink from moral obligations.*

The first is one in which citizens identify opinion leaders who appear to have views consistent with their own and then follow, in largely unthinking ways, the lead of an icon in making weighty decisions. This principle can be seen in the reliance on celebrity opinion leaders who endorse products, or in the insidious embedding of products used by celebrities in entertainment programs. Quantitatively, this principle is illustrated by studies that generally show a fairly large majority of citizens do not exercise their autonomy on social and political issues. Usually, only 30% to 35% are active in pursuing their own destinies. This number is tending to decline as the nation drifts toward the conservative. "We see a significant and growing segment of the population, especially conservatives, relying on the partisan media," according to the former president of Leigh Stowell & Co., a media and communications research and consulting firm (R. G. Barney, personal communication, May 7, 2003).

The second position is taken by individuals who, finding the world too complex to understand in the available time, select a key issue—abortion or right to life is one example—and concentrate on that issue. It is not only close to their emotional heart, but of a dichotomous nature and, therefore, easily decided.

Either of these self-reinforcing scenarios assures that individuals relying on them will narrow the focus of their information search to those with whom they agree, often isolating themselves from pluralistic media that contain the rational, fact-supported arguments that would, for a reasoning individual, produce a contributive decision. When the critical mass of individuals seeking self-reinforcing scenarios reaches a certain level, formal leaders no longer need worry about the thoughtful decision maker. Without fear of being accountable, they are able to pander to the simplistic to sway public and voter opinion.

In an ever-changing society, the need for new information never ends. Conditions today never match those of yesterday. In contrast with traditional cultures, in which one can be confident that today's rules are the same as yesterday's and that the rules have been comprehensively communicated, a dynamic society changes—if not day by day, certainly month by month and year by year. Thus, citizens in a modern society must constantly gather information and educate themselves to recognize change, adapt to it, and survive and flourish. The good health and continued well-being of their society depends on those actions.

Democracy and Education

The democratic ideal depends on an active and educated citizenry, one equipped to cope with the many obstacles to democracy. Obstacles may include steadfast commitments to established rules, powerful propaganda, or self-serving motives. Democracy asks a lot of its citizens, and it is easy for them to be led from their civic duties by their own indolence, desire to avoid conflict, resistance to change, or simply indifference. In the 1920s, Dewey (1922, 1925, 1946) argued that the solution to the challenges of democracy rests on intelligence and education, particularly education that allows for and encourages participation, discussion, and argument.

Although information may be educational, the essence of education is not found in information alone. In fact, democracy is held together not by information, but by a commitment to the shared knowledge that is a function of education based on association, communication, and understanding. Once information is accessible, the ultimate essence of education—that found in argument—can emerge. Knowledge, then, comes from dialogue and direct give-and-take. As Lasch (1990) remarked, "It is only by subjecting our preferences and projects to the test of debate that we come to understand what we know and what we still need to learn" (p. 1).

What, then, is the goal of education that has argument as its ultimate essence? Democratic theory is clear that education ought to provide all citizens with the knowledge to participate to the best of their abilities in governance of their society. Perhaps the ultimate goal of education, however, is the continuous transformation of human society. Rather than maintaining society in a fixed state, education ought to function as a process that leads to progressive social change.

If knowledge is association, communication, and understanding, a democratically organized public must have both freedom of inquiry and freedom to distribute the results of this inquiry. In other words, citizens in a democracy need a forum for articulating and debating their views. Further, this circle of debate ought to extend as widely as possible and include as many voices as possible. It is here where mass media become crucial. Media (of information, of persuasion, and of entertainment) should provide and provoke the educational mix that has as its essential quality not only information but also argument and pluralism.[1]

Journalism's Moral Obligations

The journalist as a professional is not subject to the reassuring discipline of the Professional[2] (doctor, lawyer, engineer, etc.) who is licensed, must adhere to certain standards, and may be punished or disenfranchised for transgressions. Yet, the professional obligations of journalists—moral imperatives if society is to flourish—are no less pressing than they are for the disciplined Professional. These obligations revolve around basic principles of facilitation and engagement that lie behind the reasons for distributing information.

The Obligation to Facilitate

Education happens in many places: in schools and colleges, at club meetings, in the workplace, at home, in church, in cafes, and in bars. Beyond these venues, journalism provides the best way of uniting people across our vast and complex society by keeping us both informed and connected.

Habermas (1989) introduced the notion of a bourgeois public sphere, one that developed in the coffeehouses, salons, and literary societies of 18th-century Europe. Conditions of the time allowed for a public—albeit one comprised solely of society's largely male elite—to engage in debate about public issues. Although Habermas recognized the exclusionary tendencies of a public sphere open only to a select group of individuals, he remained committed to the notion as a whole for what it could accomplish. In Habermas' public sphere both the quality, or form, of discourse and the quantity of, or openness to, popular participation are important. It is here that facts, convictions, and arguments meet, and the public engages in debate to reach conclusions that contribute to the good of the society. The question in today's society is whether media are capable of providing the kind of public sphere Habermas described.

The task is fraught with difficulties, and Habermas himself has been pessimistic about this possibility, especially in an era of mass politics, mass communication, and mass capitalism. However, many would argue that even today, a kind of media-generated public sphere is possible. Indeed, it would appear that through a Bill of Rights and more than 200 years of history, the American nation has created an environment in which journalism and the media can do just that.

If that is so, the question of morality and values is raised about journalism's (or the media's) role in affecting the public sphere. For a culture that values individual effort and the ideal outcomes of freedom and knowledge, media have a vital role and moral obligation suggested by a utilitarian end (Pojman, 1999). To fulfill this role, they have been granted special treatment in a constitutional culture. American culture relies on freedom and knowledge to produce the desired outcomes of a dynamic, democratic society; let us not forget that both freedom and knowledge are based on information.

> *Journalism promotes desirable values by ... creating a public cultural arena ... encouraging public participation.*

All media affect the development of such a society. Advertising and public relations create a vigorous arena in which contending ideas confront each other, supported by professional advocates; entertainment may contain messages that ferment social change in a benign setting. Again, because journalism is the most common element in critical discussions of media roles, we will concentrate on it, with the recognition that it represents the broad range of media activity.

Normatively speaking, journalism promotes desirable values by serving as a communication system that creates a public cultural arena. The relevant role of the press here is to encourage participation, including educating the public by providing information and fostering debate. Historically, creating a public space has been a concrete goal of many newspapers, even to the extent that the mid-19th-century *Houston Star* turned its building lobby into a public salon where citizens were encouraged to stop by to read or talk with the paper's staffers and other Houston residents (Kovach & Rosenstiel, 2001). This journalistic tradition has since waned, but the idea remains. Journalism (and media generally) in today's large-scale democracy ought to contain the equivalents of town meetings; in them, the marketplace of ideas ought to be found.

In practical terms, this means that journalists must be open to and seek input from citizens who have a real stake in the issues being discussed, not merely consulting experts and spokespeople who have become the standard sources of conventional wisdom. This is an important concept because an open, competitive system of information is characterized by universal efforts of participants to accumulate power, which is the ability to manipulate others while controlling one's own environment.

Individuals who live under systems of limited regulation tend to vie for power. If information is power, the media play a central role in its accumulation and distribution. It is this accumulation and distribution of information—a power-redistribution function—that, if done properly, insulates the media from accusations of self-interest. Often, experts and spokespeople who represent powerful interests seek to accumulate and seal power through maintaining the status quo and pressuring for adherence to accepted conventions (a framework within which those who already hold power find it easier to accumulate more power). Journalism's inclusion of the public in discussions of public concern is, therefore, critical to preventing unhealthy accumulations of power by providing the information needed to make individual decisions that, ideally, tend to challenge unworthy conventions, reducing the corrosive power of the status quo. A by-product of this is the media function of *redistributing power* and discouraging its concentration.

Involving the public does not mean simply conducting "person on the street" interviews in which a citizen is asked, for example, "Do you oppose or support the war with Iraq?" With this simplistic approach, the media often set up two extremes, usually represented by experts and spokespeople on opposite ends of the spectrum. Then, citizens are asked to take a side on an artificially polarized and oversimplified issue. From there, attention turns back to the experts and spokespeople; debate devolves into a fighting match between two extremes—neither of which represents the positions of most people—and the public finds itself disenfranchised.

Involving citizens also means more than presenting the two "official" sides of an issue and then seeking a "yes" or "no" response; there is no moral value in this type of approach. Instead—using the example of the United States and Iraq—journalists should provide a comprehensive account of the issue, not just reports of events that relate to it, such as the United Nations weapons inspectors' latest findings, a press conference by the president, a letter from Saddam Hussein, and so forth. Journalists should ask citizens what they know about the issue and what they want to know, and they should watch and listen carefully for public response, understanding that response comes in forms other than traditional news events, such as rallies or protests.

Journalists can find out what citizens have to say and encourage their participation in a number of ways. These range from news organizations asking for responses through the editorial pages of their newspapers to sponsoring public forums aimed at fostering dialogue. Journalists should also take extra efforts to ensure the participation of those who are usually absent. In this way, voice is given to the voiceless, and a public sphere that more accurately represents the public begins to develop.

The Obligation to Engage

Even if journalism embraces a philosophy of the public sphere and meets the obligation of facilitation, what is the remedy for a public that will not participate, either through lack of interest or energy? The answer is found in another obligation that journalism has toward citizens: Journalism must activate inquiry in citizens through what Dewey (1946) called a subtle, delicate, vivid, and responsive art of communication. For Dewey, journalism as art was crucial to a participatory democracy; aesthetics provide a way to move people without turning them into reasoning machines. Dewey envisioned journalism as joining the art of communication with social inquiry. In this kind of space, journalism is able to nurture the educational spirit.

In its obligation to engage citizens, journalism must strike a delicate balance between what is in the public interest and what the public is interested in. Through the years, this has provided a classic conflict. The market requires giving the public what it wants; democracy requires giving the public what it needs. How, then, are both requirements met?

> *The media's function*
> *with citizens is to orient them*
> *in an actual world and to inspire*
> *them to opt in.*

Offering a substantive definition of the public interest—one that goes further than "that which serves society's needs"—is not simple. There is no consensus; the notion of public interest is contextual across time, place, media system, and media type. Embracing a philosophy of the public sphere does, however, help the press serve the public interest by facilitating society's conversation. Responding to public demand, on the other hand, is easier to accomplish. A market-driven media system can gauge the interests of citizen consumers through ratings, circulations, and market shares, which indicate that the public, or at least a media organization's target market, is getting what it wants.

The media's function with citizens is to orient them in an actual world and to inspire them to opt in. This is the principle behind the traditional responsibilities of journalists to "afflict the comfortable and comfort the afflicted" (Ross, 2002) with information. Fulfillment of this role means contributing beyond the interests of media or of audiences alone. The goal, the desired consequence, is a democracy that works.

Citizens' Moral Obligations to Journalism and Society

In a just society in which citizen welfare is of paramount concern, citizens would appear to have at least four moral obligations to protect their standing and sovereignty in their communities. The first three are duties that depend on the professional performance of journalists, and the fourth is a corollary in which the freedoms of citizens' fountains of information (the media) need to be protected.

1. Obligation of Exposure

Citizens ought to energetically expose themselves to ideas, primarily because of their need for reliable information as a precursor to thoughtful decisions. Further, the need is for pluralistic rather than "reinforcing" or "cheerleading" information that tends to inflate the importance of the status quo.

Therefore, citizens' moral obligations transcend the collection of information and include a mandate to conscientiously absorb pluralistic information that will inform them well on all the significant facets of a given topic.

This is a significant element, because the number of people who read—particularly newspapers and magazines—seems to be in decline, suggesting that in-depth, self-informing activity is becoming more limited. A bright spot may be found in exploding Internet traffic, which suggests that significant on-line reading may be bolstering declining print reading figures. Nevertheless, online activity suggests the danger of only consulting reinforcing sources, collecting information that conforms to predispositions, prejudices, and biases, virtually eliminating pluralistic media consumption.

2. Obligation of Response

In an ideal world, each citizen would first make decisions based on a fairly precise definition of need. Following the satisfaction of needs, decisions would then turn to the use of leftover resources to satisfy wants. Although the product of nearly 300 million consumers in the United States seems to result in a fair balance of satisfied needs and wants in terms of consumer goods and services, in other areas the equation is more difficult. Beyond the economic realm, citizens must exert themselves more to provide a "vote" on a given matter, and immediate results are often not apparent. So it is with feedback to the media. One might argue that citizens should provide feedback (e.g., in the form of calls and letters to the editor) that, if it reaches a critical mass, informs the editor of community expectations and allows for adjustments in media content to fit community needs.

3. Obligation to Diversity

The feedback just discussed requires citizens to be altruistic: They must demand the unpleasant or unsettling information necessary for productive community decisions. The nature of a democratic society is one of active adversaries and advocates who constantly make their positions known to media operators. Seldom is there a balance of views from these sources, as those who have power and resources are more likely to fund efforts to influence editors in ways that will enhance that power. Editors often hear also from single-issue citizens whose demands tend to be directional. More rare is the feedback from the rational citizen who finds value in the medium, but who seeks additional coverage in certain areas to better understand the emerging environment. Such news may be disturbing or distasteful but necessary for greater understanding.

> *Diverse sources promote*
> *a pluralistic society in the face*
> *of ... a homogenization process*
> *that limits options.*

Just as many people find refuge in investing themselves in groups or leaders, or in concentrating on single issues to the detriment of social discourse, so do others confine themselves to a single medium for the bulk of their information. A rule of thumb given university journalism students is that, to maintain their moral autonomy, they must refuse to rely on only one or two news sources if they hope to write a complete story. So it is with the public. Diverse sources promote a pluralistic society in the face of trends that seem to seek a homogenization process that limits options.

However, diversifying sources is not an emotionally simple task (Rokeach, 1960). Many of us seek to minimize dissonance in our lives; one way is by regulating the inflow of our information to that which tends to comfort. Therefore, if citizens have a moral obligation to serve others by making contributive decisions, altruism demands that citizens be exposed to and absorb belief-discrepant information.

4. Protect Media Autonomy

Incessant public onslaughts against the media are facts of life, as are public appeals to discipline or discredit media in the battles for power. Reduced media credibility causes audiences to rely on opinion leaders who direct followers to specific decisions, rather than promoting pluralism and public discussion. When the public falls in with the critics, in most cases, the media feel pressures to restrict coverage and to reduce the range of views they include in stories. As only one example, the public tends to be receptive of judicial and legal communities' pressures to reduce media coverage of trials and other justice system proceedings that are supposed to be public. Such reduced coverage is of short-term benefit to the legal community (and long-term detriment to society), as it shields the processes from the very public it enlists to criticize media behavior.

Further, of course, public discussions to bring pressures on the media are conducted in the media themselves. It probably is a credit to the media that their interest in pluralism leads to discussions in the media that have the greatest impact on the media.

> *The public should defend the
> media out of valid self-interest.*

If the public defends the media out of valid self-interest (i.e., defending an institution constitutionally franchised to aid democracy), the media are able to better fulfill their other vital functions.

The Moral Basis for Reciprocity

If a participatory society depends on a reservoir of good will among its citizens, which causes them to cooperate with each for the benefit of all, such a symbiotic relation between two of the most important elements of a participatory culture—the media and the citizen—is also logical. Such an alliance, although certainly not free of adversarial overtones, speaks of reciprocal obligations in which each must, as a minimum, do its part to complement the other's role in maintaining a dynamic society. This is not a legal requirement; for a participatory society to flourish, the imposition of a minimum of legal requirements is replaced by the necessity for a number of moral obligations to which a substantial number of citizens must voluntarily subscribe. The press, for its part, must provide the information and stimulate the debate necessary for productive cumulative citizen decisions.

Citizens, at the same time, must find it in their best interest to protect the media from emotional incursions on free speech, protect the open distribution of information, and even protect the individualism that makes a free press possible. Such emotion gains intensity in times of stress, and the media and consequent social decision making abilities tend to be the first affected.

If the media fail in their jobs, history demonstrates that power will accumulate to the extent that a participatory democracy will be lost. As the American Civil Liberties Union reminds, "freedom can't protect itself" (New ACLU, 2003). If citizens fail in their responsibilities, history shows that the media are vulnerable to emotional, power seeking appeals for a more "responsible" press, a responsibility that most often means a press that reinforces community values and leads the cheers for the status quo. This makes change as impossible in a democracy as it has been in traditional cultures for generations.

When the minimum requirements are met and there exists a forum through which the public conversation can openly proceed, the work of a democratic society can truly progress. This work is not easy. Within media obligations to provide information is a mandate to include history, context, interpretation, and sufficient depth to give meaning to an issue. Stimulating debate can present even greater challenges. First, the media must present information in ways that attracts citizens; second, media must engage them to respond; and third, media must be attentive to the responses. Media must facilitate the debate they have stimulated. If these obligations are met, an effective media system is likely.

For citizens, ensuring protections of the media is also just a start. The potential of a free press is only realized when all take advantage of it by, first, seeking out the wide variety of information available on critical issues of the day—including that which may be unsettling or challenging to one's established views—and, second, responding to that information through the public forum of the media. If these obligations are met, an active public results, and media protection is perpetuated.

Most of the world's religions, whatever their concept of a god, advance a variation of the basic rule of human relations often called the Golden Rule: "Do unto others as you would have them do unto you." These range from Christian and Islamic teachings through the Buddhist "Hurt not others with that which pains yourself," to the Yorubans of Nigeria who tell adherents "One going to take a pointed stick to pinch a baby bird should first try it on himself to feel how it hurts" (The Golden Rule, 2003). Such statements confirm the durability of expressions of reciprocal obligations and of cooperative enterprise. They can surely qualify as a starting point for the exploration of a supporting reciprocal moral obligation between the mass media and the audiences they serve.

Although such a reciprocal arrangement may imply a relativist orientation—a "you scratch my back and I'll scratch yours" mentality—in fact, it is more consistent with a principled orientation in which a social contract binds us to observance of universal moral principles. The key to this orientation is emphasis on a possibility of change in the social contract, an essential element in a participatory society that tends to assure that normative standards can change as conditions and circumstances require. Sometimes those changes occur with substantial resistance and public debate. At other times, the changes emerge from frequent depictions of new standards in the news or entertainment media. Such possibility of change is largely eliminated if the citizenry is ignorant of events surrounding it. Therefore, mass media becomes a serious agent in enabling autonomous moral agents to detect the need for changes in the contract and to have means through which to work for those changes, even to the extent that the work requires violation of current standards.

A democratic society is, by nature, a teleological culture.

An assertion of likelihood of change suggests that a democratic society, by its nature, is a teleological culture, one concerned primarily with consequences and one that assumes its citizens are equal to the task of engineering measured change—the altering of nonmoral values—that assists society in adapting to new conditions (Pojman, 1999). It is important to recognize that a teleological foundation requires rational, deliberative practitioners. If the state trusts people to act rationally and validates the power of public opinion, the obligation of journalists to provide information and facilitate knowledge building becomes more pressing, as does the obligation of citizens to protect and perpetuate the channels of their knowledge.

Moral reciprocity in a democratic society is not confined to that between media and citizens. Consider, for instance, school districts in Oregon, which in January 2003 began making plans to shorten their school year by 14 days or more because of inadequate funds. These plans were announced in the face of a referendum on raising taxes to pay for schools, one that most Oregonians expected to go down in defeat and, in fact, did. The moral argument for reciprocity here is that knowledgeable, well-informed citizens—most of whom became educated through public education— have a moral obligation to reciprocate by sacrificing some of the means they gained through their education for the education of the next genera- tion (Dillon, 2003). To fail to agree to pay sufficient taxes to educate today's generation as they themselves were educated through the use of tax funds—even if this payment is a hardship—is to morally fail both the vul- nerable and innocent children and the society at large, making that society more susceptible to manipulations of demagogues and power seekers who thrive on citizen ignorance.

Consideration of ethics involves examining the use of power one exerts over another. If media do not use their power wisely, they fail those whose power is directly related to the information they receive. Similarly, citizens fail if they do not make an effort to empower themselves by taking advan- tage of the information the media provide and, consequently, preventing accumulations of power by those who thrive on ignorance.

What about those for whom access to information has been historically limited? What about the ignorant, the disempowered? Here, we see super- erogatory obligations arise for those with power to use it not only wisely but also compassionately. This requires exerting an extra effort to work toward bringing as many as possible into the realm of rational participation, to help ensure that all who are willing to spend the time and energy to participate have the means and the ability to exercise agency, to take on the moral obliga- tion of reciprocity. For it must be remembered that ultimately in a democratic society, ethics is not only consequential but is critically important to democ- racy's survival, and that which is given the highest value—the ideal toward which we all strive—is the broad social good. This good can only be defined and achieved when the ideas of all are taken into consideration.

Notes

1. Our concentration here will tend to be on journalism as the primary provider of information. However, the persuasive arts (primarily advertising and pub- lic relations) also provide valuable information to stimulate public discussion, just as entertainment media stimulate thought and social change.
2. Note the use of capital and lower case "p" in distinguishing between profes- sional classes. A Professional is one who is fairly rigorously regulated, is sub- ject to internal ethical discipline, and who is required to maintain licensure by the state (most prominent are medical doctors and lawyers). A professional, on the other hand, is expected to behave in ways that enhance the calling, and use their skills in contributive ways (librarians, teacher, professors, journal- ists, and many others), although there is no mandated obligation to do so. One of the authors is grateful, for example, that a medical orderly, a student who had protested a failing grade, acted professionally by not accidentally dump- ing or bumping his former professor on the way to surgery.

References

Dewey, J. (1922, May 3). Public opinion. *The New Republic,* pp. 286–288.

Dewey, J. (1925, December 2). Practical democracy. *The New Republic,* pp. 52–54.

Dewey, J. (1946). *The public and its problems: An essay in political inquiry* (2nd ed.). Chicago: Gateway.

Dillon, S. (2003, January 12). Oregon ending school year early to cut costs. *New York Times,* p. A-1.

Every, D. (2002, September 2). *Is Bill Gates a genius?: A history of Microsoft successes.* Retrieved April 27, 2003, from www.igeek.com/articles/history/IsBillGatesaGenius.txt

The Golden Rule. (2003). Retrieved May 18, 2003, from www.fragrant.demon.co.uk/golden.html

Habermas, J. (1989) *The structural transformation of the public sphere: An inquiry into a category of bourgeois society* (T. Burger, Trans.). Cambridge, MA: MIT Press.

Kovach, B., & Rosenstiel, T. (2001). *The elements of journalism: What newspeople should know and the public should expect.* New York: Three Rivers.

Lasch, C. (1990, Spring). Journalism, publicity and the lost art of argument. *Gannett Center Journal,* pp. 1–11.

Mill, J. (1956). *On liberty.* Indianapolis, IN: Bobbs-Merrill. (Original work published 1859)

New ACLU advertisements dramatize post-9/11 "lessons" in civil liberties. (2003, July 15). Retrieved January 16, 2004, from http://www.aclu.org/SafeandFree/SafeandFree.cfm?ID=13122&c=206

Pojman, L. (1999). *Ethics: Discovering right and wrong* (3rd ed.). Belmont, CA: Wadsworth.

Rokeach, M. (1960). *The open and closed mind.* New York: Basic Books.

Ross, D. (2002, March 7). What should reporters be? *Valley Roadrunner.* Retrieved June 2, 2003, from www.valleycenter.com/frontpage/03-07-02

Journal of Mass Media Ethics, *19*(3&4), 207–222
Copyright © 2004, Lawrence Erlbaum Associates, Inc.

The One-Sided Obligations of Journalism

Michael Davis
Illinois Institute of Technology

❏ *Barger and Barney (2004/this issue) offered a number of reasons for the public, the news media, and journalism to develop special, mutually supportive standards of conduct. However, they imbedded these reasonable suggestions in an argument that claims far more than can be delivered. In explaining what is wrong with their argument, I place journalistic ethics within a general theory of professional ethics.*

"The best is the enemy of the good."
—Voltaire

In their joint article, "Media-Citizen Reciprocity as a Moral Mandate," Wendy Barger and Ralph Barney (2004/this issue; hereafter "B&B") describe a set of relations between "journalist" and "citizen" they sometimes term an "ideal," but more often a "moral obligation" or "moral mandate." My quarrel is not with the ideal—provided we remember that ideals, even moral ideals, do not oblige or mandate precisely because the realization of one ideal tends to prevent the realization of others. Only a fanatic pursues one moral ideal to the detriment of all others. To be a perfect citizen, for example, one likely has to do some things a perfect parent or perfect scholar would not do (put the interests of the polis above those of family or truth).

Rather than quarrel with B&B's ideal, I quarrel with their claim to establish "mandates" or "obligations" (acts morally required or forbidden). I argue that their claim rests (a) in part on a failure to appreciate what a moral argument must be but (b) in part too on a failure to appreciate the power (and limits) of arguments relying on professional ethics. I conclude with a few remarks about how to use what I have done.

Two Kinds of Argument From Reciprocity

By "reciprocity," B&B seem to mean two quite different moral relations, what we might distinguish as "natural" and "conventional." For much of their article, the moral obligations that concern them seem to be natural ones, obligations arising from "the nature of things" ("teleology"). So, for example, they assert, "For a participatory society to flourish, the imposition of a minimum of legal requirements is replaced by the necessity for a number of moral obligations to which ... citizens must voluntarily subscribe" (Barger & Barney, 2004/this issue, pp. 202–203).

The claim that certain facts—such as "participatory society cannot flourish [without such and such an obligation being imposed]" means there is a moral obligation to do such and such—is an appeal to nature rather than convention. One's "natural obligations" derive not from one's own voluntary acts, as contractual obligations generally do, but simply from standing in a certain relation to another (say, in the relation of beneficiary to benefactor). For much of their article, B&B seem to be concerned with the nature of things (democracy, media, and citizen), deriving their "mandates" from the inevitable relations among these entities. For this part of the article, "reciprocity" seems to be equivalent to "mutual dependence" (or "mutual advantage").

Elsewhere (even in the previous quote), B&B talk in ways that eventually lead them to interpret reciprocity as a "social contract" (something to which citizens "voluntarily subscribe"). For example, they assert, "a social contract binds us to observance of universal moral principles" (Barger & Barney, 2004/this issue, p. 204). As I understand this passage, the benefits citizens receive from certain "universal principles" come as part of an exchange for certain conduct (following those same principles). The conduct in question is ordinary moral conduct (what the universal principles of morality ask). Yet, according to B&B, citizens cannot claim the benefits of those universal principles simply as human persons. Citizens must (they say) enter the contract to have those benefits—and, presumably, have the option of not entering and so, the option of being (properly) treated as less than human.

B&B offer no argument for their assumption that society has a moral right to withhold the benefits in question. Indeed, it is hard to see how they could offer such an argument without recognizing in society rights more totalitarian than most of us would find defensible. Human beings in general, and therefore citizens in particular, have rights everyone, including government, is bound to respect. Some of these, such as the right to be treated as a person, are not rights we can waive or renounce; we have them while we remain human persons. B&B's argument from convention thus seems bound to fail. There can be no actual social contract, no convention, without a voluntary exchange of benefits. However, there can be no voluntary exchange of benefits where society has no right to withhold what it is supposed to grant in exchange for something else. There can also be no social contract, no convention of any sort, where the mutual obligations are necessary, that is, where they exist independent of any convention. Convention is an act of will, not a natural relation.

Convention is an act of will,
not a natural relation.

To make their convention argument work, B&B would have to show that society has a right to withhold the benefits in question. What B&B do, instead, is show how those benefits depend (in part) on some citizens (or "the public") acting in certain ways (the ways B&B claim citizens have a moral obligation to act), for example, reading the news thoughtfully. Instead of appealing to promises or other means of creating a convention, they appeal to general moral principles (such as the Golden Rule) to establish the obligation. Appeal to "social contract" where the exchange is not voluntary seems both at odds with their simultaneous appeal to nature and a serious mistake in itself (though one common in the history of social contract as an explanation of political obligation).[1]

I shall therefore ignore B&B's conventional argument hereafter. We must now consider how, according to B&B, the reciprocal moral obligations of media and public are supposed to arise from nature.

Immediately, we confront a problem. How are we to tell what is and what is not a moral standard? This is not an idle question. One of B&B's arguments appeals to "most of the world's religions" for the "basic rule of human relations often called the Golden Rule: 'Do unto others as you would have them do unto you'." B&B go on to reason, "[Such statements] can surely qualify as a starting point for the exploration of a supporting reciprocal moral obligation between the mass media and the audiences they serve" (Barger & Barney, 2004/this issue, p. 204).

This appeal to religion is doubly troubling. The first trouble is factual. As far as I can determine, Christianity is the only religion to endorse the Golden Rule. What the others seem to endorse (even those B&B quote) is what is sometimes called "the Silver Rule," "Do not do to others what you don't want them to do to you."[2] The difference between the Golden Rule and Silver Rule is not merely verbal. The Golden Rule asks us to do something positive, indeed, to do lots of things for others, everything we want them to do for us. It is a hard rule to satisfy. Even a Good Samaritan may fail to do all the Golden Rule asks. In contrast, the Silver Rule asks only that we abstain from doing to others what we do not want to suffer ourselves. We can obey the Silver Rule while asleep. We need do nothing.

So, that is one trouble with B&B's appeal to religion. Religions differ just where B&B claim unanimity. The second trouble, the more important, is that religious rules are not necessarily moral rules. (Consider, for example, a rule against eating pork or mandating that a tenth of one's income be given to church or charity.) So, even if all religions of the world were (more or less) unanimous in their endorsement of some rule, we could not conclude from that unanimity that the rule is a moral rule (or even that it could "found" a moral rule). B&B need an analysis of morality, one not only capable of distinguishing the moral from the religious but one capable of determining whether the rules of interest to them are moral rules—or just moral ideals or even something morally indifferent. I shall now provide such an analysis—or, rather, sketch enough of such an analysis to allow us to determine whether the reciprocal obligations that B&B identify are indeed moral obligations. That sketch should contain no surprises.

Morality

By *morality*, I shall mean those standards of conduct everyone—that is, every rational person at her rational best—wants everyone else to be subject to, even if that means she too must be subject to them. Morality, so defined, is personal insofar as each person (at her rational best) has a veto. Nothing can be morality unless each person wants it to be a universal standard of conduct. Morality so defined is, however, also objective (or, at least, intersubjective). Nothing can be morality unless every person (at her rational best) wants it. Morality, though personal to each, is a common possession of all.

The twin tests of unanimity and rationality together provide a standard of practical justification. The test of unanimity assures that morality will be something that those subject to its standards will take an interest in. That interest means every moral agent will always have a reason to act morally—though not necessarily a decisive reason. The test of rationality (that each person at her rational best endorses the standard) assumes as well that morality is a rational undertaking. A person is at her rational best if she would still want what she wants now were she to be exposed to all relevant information in a lively, understandable, and accurate way. Rationality (in this sense) seems to be (more or less) equivalent to what B&B call individual (moral) autonomy.[3]

The twin tests of unanimity and rationality have an important consequence. There is an asymmetry in the justification of moral standards. We are in a much better position to show that a certain proposed standard is not a moral standard than to show that it is. We can show that a proposed standard is not a moral standard simply by producing one person who (at her rational best) does not want everyone else to be subject to the standard or at least does not want that so much that she would be willing to be subject to it if her subjection to it were the price of all others being so subject. In contrast, we cannot show that a standard is a moral standard by producing one person who wants the standard so much that she would be willing to be subject to it if that is the price of all others being so subject. We can only provide reasons to think that everyone would want everyone else to be subject to the standard even if their subjection meant she too would be subject to it. We must recognize that we can underestimate the variety in what rational persons (at their rational best) in fact want.

Morality, so defined, has a certain resemblance to the Golden Rule. We are invited to consider what we want others to do, to determine what we should do. This resemblance may explain much of the Golden Rule's appeal. However, for our purposes, what is important is how morality so defined differs from the Golden Rule. There are at least two differences worth noting. First, the Golden Rule allows each person to decide what is required of him by considering what he would like others to do. He need not consider whether anyone else agrees with him. The definition of morality proposed here does require him to consider that. The Golden Rule may therefore lead to actions quite different from those morality leads to.

Second, the Golden Rule does not (explicitly) require that one's own desires, the sole measure of how one is to treat others, be rational. The Golden Rule is therefore open to counter-examples involving bizarre desires (or beliefs). For example, if I believe this world to be vale of tears and wish someone would put me out of my misery, the Golden Rule will seem to oblige me to kill anyone who asks me to and perhaps even just anyone who is unhappy. In contrast, morality as I defined it does not even seem to have that consequence because (a) it excludes irrational beliefs and desires and (b) it requires that everyone want the standard, not just one odd person.

Actual morality binds us,
but ideal morality merely offers
terms of exhortation, grounds for
criticism of existing moral rules.

Morality, though justified, may still be either actual or ideal. Actual morality consists of those justified standards actually in place in our society; ideal morality, of those standards we endorse when we ignore the costs of changing current practice. Actual morality is, in part, a product of historical accident in a way ideal morality is not. Nonetheless, actual morality binds us, but ideal morality merely offers terms of exhortation, grounds for criticism of existing moral rules (however justified now), and so a basis for planning the future.

Morality is a set of standards. Standards, even the standards of actual morality, are not laws of nature in the way the laws of physics are. Moral agents can choose not to follow actual moral standards. Indeed, whenever people talk about morality (or, indeed, about any standard of conduct), we can draw two conclusions. One is that people sometimes do not follow those standards. (If everyone always did follow the standard, we would count it among the "laws of nature," not as a standard of conduct.) The other is that they do not so often that there is no point to drawing attention to the standard. Any discussion of (actual) morality presupposes both good news (a widespread social approximation of morality) and bad news (a significant number of contrary acts).

Whether actual or ideal, there are at least three kinds of moral standard: rules, principles, and ideals.

A moral rule requires (or forbids) a course of action. "Don't kill" and "Keep your promises" are moral rules. Rules have exceptions. For example, "self-defense" is an exception to "Don't kill." To fail to do what a rule requires (or to do what a rule forbids) is wrong, unless justified under some exception. Rules lay down relatively rigid standards of conduct. Even when disobeying the rule is justified, the disobedience may leave behind liability to make good any harm one caused. Because rules are relatively demanding, we should expect there to be relatively few moral rules. The writer from whom I have taken much of this analysis of moral rules, Bernard Gert (1988), identified 10 moral rules. Perhaps there are a few more or a few less.

Moral principles, in contrast, do not concern conduct directly. They merely require certain considerations to have a certain weight in our deliberations.[4] They state reasons. For example, "Help the needy" does not require us to give charity whenever we can but to consider the needs of the needy when we are making allocations. Principles are primarily standards of deliberation. Because it is easier to give the appropriate weight to a consideration than to do what a rule requires, there are many more principles than rules.[5]

Moral ideals do something more complex. Like rules, they are directly concerned with conduct; but, like principles, they do not require any particular conduct. Instead, they present the conduct in question as a state of affairs good to try for or approach but not bad to ignore or fall short of. The injunction, "Be a Good Samaritan," is commonly thought to state a moral ideal. Moral ideals are morally important insofar as they give others a reason to help, reward, or at least praise those who try to realize a particular ideal.[6]

The "Golden Rule" seems to be a principle or ideal, not a rule, if it is a moral standard at all. Hence, it cannot tell us what acts are morally required. For that reason, we cannot derive a moral obligation of reciprocity from it. B&B's appeal to the Golden Rule is a mistake.

Perhaps the rule B&B actually have in mind is not the Golden Rule but a standard much less demanding. I can think of only three possibilities consistent with what they say: One is gratitude ("Benefit those who benefit you"); another is the involuntary version of the "principle of fairness" ("Obey the rules of any morally permissible cooperative practice from which you benefit when the benefit to others depends in part on your obeying the rules just as they do"); and the third is prudence. The problem with these three standards is that none is a moral rule, though each fails for a somewhat different reason.

"Obligations of gratitude" are not obligations strictly speaking; they are more like considerations we should take into account. We should, all else equal, try to benefit those who benefit us. To fail to take into account the welfare of those who benefit us is to exhibit ingratitude. However, merely to fail to benefit those who benefit us is not generally ingratitude. As long as we have good reason for what we do, even if just the disproportion between the small benefit we would return and the large cost of bestowing it, we do all that gratitude requires. Gratitude is a principle, not a rule, because a rule requiring gratitude would be too demanding. We would rather do without the benefits of gratitude than suffer the demands a rule of gratitude would impose. We can get most of the benefits of gratitude from a principle while avoiding the substantial burdens of a rule.

The involuntary version of the principle of fairness seems to fail as a moral rule for a somewhat different reason. It would allow others to draft us into their (morally permissible) practices simply by including us in the benefits deriving from those practices, whether we want the benefits or not. We can obtain most of the benefits of the principle of fairness by accepting the involuntary form as a principle rather than a rule while accepting as a rule the voluntary form (i.e., one making voluntary acceptance of benefits the basis of obligation). From the involuntary form of the "principle of fairness" (a true principle) we cannot derive any moral obligation; from the voluntary form (a true rule) we can derive a moral obligation, but only where there is a certain convention. Either way, fairness will not allow a moral obligation to be derived from nature.

By "prudence" I mean those standards of conduct everyone (at her rational best) wants to follow, whether others do the same or not. Like morality, prudence is a standard of conduct. However, although morality is concerned with how we should act as part of a common enterprise, prudence is concerned with how we should act even if there is no common enterprise. We want others to be moral even if we are not. We want to be prudent even if no one else is. Prudence is the complement of morality. Hence, we cannot derive moral standards from considerations of prudence alone. B&B are simply mistaken when, for example, they claim: "It would seem unassailable that consumers have a moral obligation—both to themselves and to their community—to spend their money in ways that will be of mutual benefit and will not unjustly enrich vendors for inferior products" (Barger & Barney, 2004/this issue, p. 193).

Prudence does require consumers to spend their money in ways that will benefit them and not unjustly enrich vendors for inferior products.

Why waste money? However, no moral obligation follows from that. Indeed, the opposite would seem to follow. Prudence makes it unnecessary to have a moral rule requiring us to look after our own interests, leaving us with no reason to burden ourselves with such a rule. That others are also, in general, prudent makes it equally unnecessary to have a moral rule requiring them to look after their own interests.

B&B seem to face a dilemma. To have the moral mandate they seek, they need a moral rule from which to derive it. Standards from which they could derive the mandate are too demanding to be moral rules. Those standards that are moral rules, being less demanding, do not allow for derivation of the mandate. B&B's "reciprocity" seems to be a dead end. It is time to consider an alternative.

Ethics as a (Partial) Alternative to Reciprocity

B&B attempted to explain the moral mandate of news media (or, at least, journalists) as deriving from ordinary moral rules together with certain facts about the media, citizens, and society, what I have called an explanation "from nature." What I propose to do now is to offer an explanation resting on convention. I like to think of this explanation as ethical rather than moral. To avoid confusion, I need to explain what I have in mind by that contrast. After all, *ethics* has at least five senses in ordinary English. In one, it is a mere synonym for ordinary morality, those universal standards of conduct that were the subject of the preceding section. Etymology fully justifies that first sense. The root for *ethics* (*ethos*) is the Greek word for custom, just as the root of *morality* (*mores*) is the Latin word for it. Etymologically, *ethics* and *morality* are twins (as are *ethic* and *morale*). In this first sense of *ethics*, the contrast between ethics and morality makes no sense. That cannot be the sense of *ethics* I need here.

Ethics, in four other senses, can be contrasted with morality. In one, ethics is said to consist of those standards of conduct that moral agents should follow (what is sometimes also called "critical morality"); morality, in contrast, is said to consist of those standards that moral agents actually follow ("positive morality"). *Morality* in this sense is very close to its root, *mores*; it can be unethical (in our first sense of ethics). Morality (in this sense) has a plural; each society or group can have its own moral code, indeed, even each individual can have her own. There can be as many moralities as there are moral agents. However, even so, ethics remains a standard common to everyone (or, at least, may be such a standard, depending on how "critical morality" gets cashed out). *Ethics* in this sense is equivalent to the first sense I identified; it is *morality* that has changed. This is still not the sense of *ethics* I need.

Ethics is sometimes contrasted with morality in another way. Morality then consists of those standards every moral agent should follow. Morality is a universal minimum, our standard of moral right and wrong. Ethics, in contrast, is concerned with moral good, with whatever is beyond the moral minimum. Ethics (in this sense) is whatever is left over of morality (in our first—universal—sense, which includes both the right and the good) once we subtract morality (in this third—minimum right-only—sense). Because B&B suppose (and I agree) that media ethics, whatever it turns out to be, consists (in large part at least) of moral requirements ("mandates"), this third sense cannot be the one needed here.

This "should" sense of ethics is closely related to another, the sense it has when used for a field of philosophy. When philosophers offer a course in ethics, or say they specialize in ethics, they refer to a discipline concerned with understanding morality (all or part of morality in our first sense) as a rational undertaking. Philosophers do not teach morality (in our first, second, or third sense)—except perhaps by inadvertence. They also generally do not teach critical morality, though the attempt to understand morality as a rational undertaking should lead students to dismiss some parts of morality (in its second, descriptive, sense) as irrational or to feel more committed to morality (in its first or third sense) because they can now see the point of it. This is another sense of *ethics* in which ethics does not consist (even in part) of mandates (though it does consist in part of the study of mandates). This then is also a sense of *ethics* not needed here.

How is it possible for the media (or the public) to have special moral responsibilities?

Last, *ethics* can be used to refer to those special, morally permissible standards of conduct governing members of a group simply because they are members of that group. In this sense, Hopi ethics are for Hopi and for no one else; engineering ethics, for engineers and for no one else; and media ethics, for people in the media and for no one else. Ethics—in this sense—is relative, even though morality is not. However, ethics (in this sense) is not therefore mere mores. Ethics must—by definition—be morally permissible. There can be no thieves' ethics or Nazi ethics, except with scare quotes around "ethics."

This last sense of *ethics* is, I think, the one implied in the claim that the media (and their publics) have a moral mandate, special responsibilities or obligations, others do not. However, so interpreted, this claim raises the question: How is it possible for the media (or the public) to have special moral responsibilities or obligations? Should not morality apply to all equally? How is media ethics possible?

My answer is that the (news) media (and their publics) can have special obligations if those obligations derive from a convention they (in fact) voluntarily enter. Such a convention is possible. Some parts of the media have, in fact, entered into such conventions. For example, the *Wall Street Journal* has announced a code of ethics for its employees. The *Journal* thereby invites readers to rely on what they read in the *Journal* because what the *Journal* publishes (apart from ads, letters to the editor, and the like) is the result of the announced process. Readers are entitled to expect the *Journal* to publish stories because of their value as news, to take care that statements are accurate, and to avoid or disclose conflicts of interest. Readers can justifiably rely on the *Journal* to do what the announced rules promise. The code is a convention (a sort of warrant or contract). Had the *Journal* announced different rules, readers could not justifiably rely on the *Journal* to do as the rules now require. The rules are an act of will; they cannot be derived from the nature of things.

Though a media-wide code of ethics like the *Journal*'s is possible, it seems to me unlikely. The "media," even the "news media," are a motley assortment of institutions. Among their members (beside the *Journal*) are the *New York Review of Books, Chicago Reader,* WGN Radio, CNN, *Southern Living, People* Magazine, and various supermarket tabloids. What standards, beyond ordinary morality, could even these few news media agree on?

Without a media-wide code, it is hard to see what readers, viewers, or listeners could get from promising the news media as a whole anything. Indeed, even if a nontrivial media-wide code were possible, there would remain the problem of discovering what the media could ask of all readers, viewers, and listeners that they would be willing to give in exchange for what a media code of ethics could offer. After all, right now, some of these media cannot even get their audience to pay for what the medium does. They live entirely on advertising, distributing their work free to any who accept it. These media are content if their readers, viewers, or listeners take the time to read, view, or listen to some of what is presented (especially, the advertisements).

Not a Media Mandate but the Profession of Journalism

Here, I think, is the place to distinguish between two sorts of ethics (in my special-standards sense): institutional and professional. An institution is a place where two or more occupations work together. Institutional ethics are the ethics of such a place. Business ethics, research ethics, and sports ethics are all examples of institutional ethics. Media ethics also seems to be a kind of institutional ethics.

What then is "professional ethics?" That, of course, depends on what we mean by *profession*. Unfortunately, *profession* resembles *ethics* in having several senses. *Profession* can, for example, be used as a mere synonym for *occupation*—an occupation being any typically full-time activity, defined in part by an easily recognizable body of knowledge, skill, and judgment (a discipline), by which one can earn a living. It is in this sense that we may, without irony, speak of someone being a "professional thief." *Profession* can, instead, be used for any occupation one may openly acknowledge or profess, that is, an honest occupation: "Plumbing is a profession; thieving is not." *Profession* can also be used for a special kind of honest occupation.

There are at least two approaches to defining this special kind of honest occupation. One approach, what we may call "the sociological," has its origin in the social sciences. Its language tends to be statistical, that is, the definition does not purport to give necessary or sufficient conditions for some occupation being a profession but merely to report what is true of "most professions," "the most important professions," or the like. Generally, sociological definitions understand a profession to be any occupation whose practitioners enjoy high social status, high income, advanced education, important social function, or other features easy for the social sciences to measure. For social scientists, there is no important distinction between what used to be called "the liberal professions" (those honest occupations requiring a knowledge of Latin and Greek) and today's professions (strictly so called). So, according to the sociologists, plumbing cannot be a profession because both the social status and education of plumbers are too low. Law certainly is a profession, because lawyers have relatively high status, high income, and advanced education. Business managers probably also form a profession (in this sense), because they too tend to have high income, high status, advanced education, and important social function. For the sociological definition, journalism is less a "probable" profession than management, because its income, social status, and education are even less than management's.

The other approach to defining "profession" is philosophical. A philosophical definition attempts a statement of necessary and sufficient conditions for an occupation to count as a profession. Although a philosophical definition may leave the status of a small number of would-be professions unsettled, it should at least be able to explain (in a satisfying way) why those would-be professions are neither clearly professions nor clearly not professions. What follows is such a philosophical definition, the product of many years trying to fit the definition to the practice that members of professions take themselves to be engaged in:

> A profession is a number of individuals in the same occupation voluntarily organized to earn a living by openly serving a moral ideal in

a morally permissible way beyond what law, market, and morality would otherwise require.[7]

According to this definition, a profession is a group undertaking. There can be no profession of one. The group must share a common occupation. (So, for example, a group consisting of physicians and lawyers cannot form a profession, though lawyers can form one profession and physicians another.) The group must organize its occupation to work in a morally permissible way. Where there is no morally permissible way to carry on the occupation, there can be no profession. There can, for example, be no profession of torturers or assassins. The organization must set standards beyond what the law, market, and ordinary morality would otherwise require. That is, the organization must set special standards. Otherwise the occupation would remain nothing more than another honest occupation. These special standards will be ethical (in the special-standards sense of ethics). They will apply to all members of the group simply because they are members of that group (and to no one else).

> *If journalists seek to facilitate public discussion and engagement, journalism pursues what at least seems a defensible moral ideal.*

More interesting, I think, is that these standards will be morally binding on every member of the profession, simply because of membership in the profession. Though the definition does not say this, this conclusion is implicit: Each profession is designed to serve a certain moral ideal, that is, to contribute to a state of affairs everyone (every rational person at her rational best) can recognize as good (that is, as what she wants to take place), good enough that she is willing to help, reward, or at least praise those who pursue it (in appropriate ways). So, physicians have organized to cure the sick, comfort the dying, and protect the healthy from disease; lawyers, to help people obtain justice within the law; accountants, to represent financial information in ways both useful and accurate; and so on. All else equal, we all want people to be healthier, to have more justice under law, to have more useful and accurate financial information, and so on. If, as B&B claim, journalists seek to facilitate public discussion and engagement, journalism pursues what at least seems a defensible moral ideal. All else equal, facilitating public discussion and engagement is a good thing.

These moral ideals must be pursued openly; that is, physicians must declare themselves to be physicians, lawyers must declare themselves to be lawyers, accountants must declare themselves to be accountants, and so on. The members of a (would-be) profession must declare themselves to be members of that profession to earn their living by that profession. They cannot be hired as such-and-such (say, a lawyer) unless they let people know that they are such-and-such. If their profession has a good reputation for what it does, their declaration of membership will aid them in earning a living. People will seek their help. If, however, their profession has a bad reputation ("I am a shyster"), their declaration of membership will be a disadvantage. People will shun their help. In general, if the members of an occupation are free to declare themselves or not, they will declare themselves only if the declaration benefits them overall (i.e., serves some purpose of their own at what seems a reasonable cost).

Where members of a (would-be) profession declare their membership voluntarily, their way of pursuing the profession's moral ideal will be a moral obligation. They will, that is, have entered a voluntary, morally permissible cooperative practice (by declaring their membership in the profession—"I am a lawyer"). They will be in position to have the benefits of the practice, employment as a member of that profession, because the employer sought a so-and-so and they declared themselves to be one. They will also be in position to take advantage of the practice by doing less than the standards of the practice require, even though the expectation that they would do what the standards require (because they declared that profession) is part of what won them employment. If cheating consists of violating the rules of a voluntary, morally permissible cooperative practice (that is, violating the voluntary form of the "principle of fairness"), then every member of a profession is in a position to cheat. With certain exceptions, it is morally wrong to cheat, every member of a profession has a moral obligation, with certain exceptions, to do as the special standards of the profession require.

Professional ethics—the special standards of the profession—imposes moral obligations. These obligations may, and generally do, vary from profession to profession (just as the obligations arising from a promise vary with what was promised). The special standards of a profession generally appear in a range of documents, including standards of admission, practice, and discipline. A code of ethics is, however, a central feature of a profession. In the United States at least, the publication of a formal code of ethics is generally the signal that an occupation has organized itself as a profession. An occupation's status as a profession is (more or less) independent of license, state-imposed monopoly, or other special legal intervention. Some professions, such as law or medicine, cannot be practiced without a license; some professions, such as engineering or psychology, require a license certain limited purposes; and some professions, such as university teaching or certified financial analysis, require no license at all.

Although professions often commit themselves to obey the law, they need not. Indeed, insofar as the laws of a particular country are unjust (or otherwise fall below the moral minimum), any provision of a professional code purporting to bind members of the profession to obey the law would be void (just as a promise to do what morality forbids is void).

Profession so understood is what B&B call "profession" (with a small "p"; Barger & Barney, 2004/this issue, p. 205). Journalism seems to me (clearly) to be a profession (in this sense). Although news media employ reporters, photographers, editors, designers, managers, lawyers, accountants, printers, machinists, guards, and even engineers, among others, only some of these employees claim to belong to a profession. Journalists are among those who do. Generally, their employer hires them as journalists (rather than as writers, storytellers, news gatherers, or the like) because "journalist" promises something other occupational descriptions do not.

If we consult a code of ethics for journalists (whether that of the Society of Professional Journalists or some other), we will find many, if not all, of the mandates B&B argue that the media have. Although the media as a whole does not seem to have such moral obligations, certain employees of some of the news media, journalists, do. Why? Because they voluntarily claim to be journalists, and part of being a journalist, rather than a mere reporter or newsperson, is (according to journalists themselves) to have these special obligations. Journalists, through their professional societies, have announced those special standards. Others, including both the public and their employers, are therefore entitled to rely on journalists to act according to those standards. Any journalist who does not wish to be relied on in this way can, and should, make clear that he is unethical (in the special-standards sense) or that he is not a journalist but a mere story writer, reporter, or the like. However, absent such a declaration, others are entitled to rely on him to be ethical (in the special-standards sense)—that is, to follow journalism's code of ethics—because he claims to be a journalist.

Journalism ethics so understood is reciprocal in a way, that is, the result of a (morally permissible) cooperative practice among journalists. However, this is not the sort of reciprocity that B&B argue for. Their reciprocity is between the media (including journalists) and the public. They seem to think their way of deriving special standards for an institution or profession is novel, as well as effective. I have already explained why it cannot be effective. I think a bit of history shows that it is far from novel. That history is also further evidence against the effectiveness of their approach.

Here is a section of the "Introduction to the Code of Ethics" adopted by the American Medical Association (AMA) in 1847:

Every duty or obligation implies, both in equity and for its successful discharge, a corresponding right. As it is the duty of a physician to advise, so has he a right to be attentively and respectfully listened to. Being required to expose his health and life for the benefit of the community, he has a just claim, in return, on all its members, collectively and individually, for aid to carry out his measures, and for all possible tenderness and regard to preventing needlessly harassing calls on his services and unnecessary exhaustion of his benevolent sympathies. (Baker, 1999, pp. 317–318)

According to the AMA of 1847, the public ("the community") has obligations to the physician because, but only because, (a) having those obligations is "equitable," that is, just or fair (in the involuntary sense of "fairness"), and (b) the public's obligations are necessary for the physician to perform his obligations. These reasons are, it seems to me, much the same as those B&B offer. It is therefore worth noting that, by 1903 the AMA had dropped all mention of the obligations of public (and patient) from its code of ethics—and, as far as I can tell, no profession now has a code of ethics suggesting reciprocal obligations between it and the public. Professionals voluntarily take on certain moral obligations without seeking to draft the public into that undertaking. The idea of reciprocal relations depending on the nature of an occupation and those who benefit from it seems to belong to an early stage in conceptualizing professional obligation (Baker, 1999).

B&B's Arguments Revisited

I am a philosopher, an outsider to journalism. As I understand philosophy, its job is to clarify. Philosophy rearranges what we believe but do not understand until it makes sense, sense enough for us to distinguish between what we should believe and what we should not. That is all I have tried to do here. I have provided what I believe to be useful distinctions, identified certain mistaken ways of arguing, and outlined an alternative at once overlooked and familiar. If I have done what I set out to do, you should now see that much of what B&B said, when properly understood, is a contribution to helping journalists, the media, and the public decide how each should act ("should" carrying a force less, much less, than "moral mandate" or "moral obligation"). B&B's arguments offer considerations to be taken into account in deciding what journalists, the media, and the public should do. B&B's chief mistake, serious but not fatal, was to think they could deduce obligations from existing or ideal relations among journalist, the media, and the public—when all they could, or did, do was offer reasons to be weighed with others as part of developing appropriate standards for the profession, for the media, and (however unlikely) for the public.

Notes

1. See, for example, Davis (2002a).
2. Some religions, such as Shinto, seem to offer no moral guidance whatever.
3. For more on what "rational best" might mean, see Davis (1987, p. 237).
4. This distinction between rules and principles seems to go back no further than Dworkin (1977, pp. 14–80).
5. So, on this analysis, what Ross (1930) called *prima facie duties* are principles; an "all things considered" judgment, a weighing up of principles. The result of such a weighing up, though a duty in some sense, is not a moral obligation (as I am using that term here). Our concern is not with any considerations relevant to determining what to do but with requirements (which differ from Ross's all-things-considered judgments in not necessarily being final determinations).
6. For more on my views on moral theory, see Davis (1992). I don't think anything I say in this article depends on accepting this view in particular. I use it simply because I prefer it to any other.
7. For a defense, see Davis (2002b).

References

Baker, R. (1999). *The American medical ethics revolution.* Baltimore: Johns Hopkins University Press.

Barger, W., & Barney, R. (2004). Media-citizen reciprocity as a moral mandate. *Journal of Mass Media Ethics, 19,* 191–206

Davis, M. (1987). Realistic utilitarianism and the social conditions of cognitive psychotherapy. *Social Theory and Practice, 13,* 237.

Davis, M. (1992). The moral legislature: Contractualism without an Archimedean point. *Ethics, 102,* 303–318

Davis, M. (2002a). *Actual social contract and political obligation: A philosopher's history through Locke.* New York: Edwin Mellen.

Davis, M. (2002b). *Profession, code, and ethics.* Aldershot, England: Ashgate.

Dworkin, R. (1977). *Taking rights seriously.* Cambridge, MA: Harvard University Press.

Gert, B. (1988). *Morality: A new justification of the moral rules.* New York: Oxford University Press.

Ross, W. (1930). *The right and the good.* London: Oxford University Press.

Journal of Mass Media Ethics, *19*(3&4), 223–246
Copyright © 2004, Lawrence Erlbaum Associates, Inc.

Power, Ethics, and Journalism: Toward an Integrative Approach

Peggy J. Bowers
Clemson University

Christopher Meyers
University of California-Bakersfield

Anantha Babbili
Middle Tennessee State University

❏ *Although we think 1 of the basic purposes of journalism is to provide information vital to enhancing citizen autonomy, we also see this goal as being in direct tension with the power news media hold and wield, power that may serve to undercut, rather than enhance, citizen autonomy. We argue that the news media are ethically constrained by proceduralism, resulting in journalists asserting power inappropriately at the individual level, and unwittingly surrendering moral authority institutionally and globally. Anonymity, institutionalization, and routinization cloak power relationships among citizens, journalists and the institutions of which they are a part, ultimately inculcating these distinctly Western values in the global community.*

Every day, at breakfast, we face the question at the door: What's up? What's new? What strange turns has the world taken since yesterday? The media tell us and commentators advise us on how to interpret the day's explosive events. Framing our day, the media wield an extraordinary power. (May, 2001, p. 205)

May's comment sits in a backdrop of an interesting shift in U.S. news culture. On the one hand, as May suggested, news media are still tremendously powerful; yet many reporters, editors, and producers feel downtrodden, stripped of their influence. They feel, in May's (2001) terms, *marginal* and *beleaguered*. Is this an accurate assessment of news media's current standing? We think not.

We grant that media power has shifted. Fewer people read the newspaper every day. Excepting times of national crisis, fewer people watch the evening news. Web-based news sources, with widely ranging levels of competency, appear to cut into mainstream news market and impact. Also, fewer people trust the news they do read, watch, and hear. All this undoubtedly affects the media's abilities to shape local, regional, and national agendas.

Even conceding these points, however, we believe news media still retain tremendous power. Seeing, though, where it resides necessitates a different kind of analysis, one that looks at the structural foundations of journalistic activities and their concomitant effects. Further, we believe this power has important ethical implications, ones not often discussed in the literature. In fact, most of the literature focuses on how news media, by providing vital information, enhance citizen autonomy and power. We want, instead, to consider ways news media power serves to undercut autonomy, as well as being the source for a range of other moral harms.

In what follows, we examine journalistic power at three levels: the microlevel, as in relationships between reporters and news subjects or sources; the institutional or professional level, as in media impact on regional political or cultural agendas; and the social level, as in media contribution to establishing and maintaining ideology. We see this as a first exploration, one that raises more issues than we can address, but we hope to provide a catalyst for additional research. It is also an exploration that has been underway in other professions for quite some time and we use those discussions, noting appropriate differences, as our guide.

Before getting at the heart of the article, we need to deal with a couple of preliminary concerns. First, a definition: Power is the ability to implement one's agenda, often, though not always, by successfully manipulating others.[1] Power, thus, admits of multiple layers—personal, group, institutional, professional, social, and cultural—and is constructed or reinforced "moment-by-moment during interaction, with all participants being involved as either its claimers or its ratifiers" (Ainsworth-Vaughn, 1998, p. 42). Furthermore, power is, as Parsons (1951) put it, "inherently diffuse," embedded in and revealed through "the variables of the social system" (p. 551), as through institutional structures and relations. Thus, to understand power's presence and impact, one must examine those variables so as to determine how their essential features serve to create, maintain, and enhance power dynamics and asymmetries.

Second, why is power of ethical concern? We take as given that autonomy (having, rationally choosing, and being able to act upon options consistent with the development of one's life-plans and character[2] and beneficence (promoting others' well-being) are foundational moral principles, ones all persons have a prima facie obligation to promote. Power, as the ability to implement one's agenda, is thus directly linked to the promotion of autonomy; powerful agents have greater opportunity to act upon those choices they deem important to the development of character. However, by the same token, power can also be wielded to restrict others' similar choices; that is, power can be used to coerce or constrain, as well as to withhold information vital to autonomous decision making. Power can also certainly be wielded to enhance others' well being or to severely damage it; one can, obviously, use position and authority to provide others with goods or to cause them great harm.

In a strict theoretical sense, power is ... ethically neutral; how it is used determines its moral value.

In a strict theoretical sense, power is thus ethically neutral; how it is used determines its moral value. However, too much of human history shows that, in practice, significant power asymmetries are nearly always ethically problematic. The less symmetrically power is held between or among persons, the more likely it is that it will undercut, rather than enhance, core moral values.

Power and Microlevel Relationships

Scholars in professional ethics, especially in medical and legal ethics, have for some years now looked at the impact of power on professional client relationships. In medicine, the focus has been primarily on the ways power asymmetries disrupt informed consent, the decision-making process necessary for promoting patient autonomy.[3]

The *idealized* model describes informed consent as a negotiated process between equals. The physician provides the information necessary for an autonomous choice—diagnosis, reasonable treatment alternatives, risks, benefits, and so forth—and the patient freely selects the option most consistent with her life plans and with what the physician's conscience allows.

The *realized* model recognizes that, in actuality, physicians make choices and patients merely assent to them. That is, because physicians hold most of the power, they determine what should be done and patients simply go along. This asymmetry exists because of realities on both sides: Physicians have specialized knowledge and skills, they use a technical language inaccessible to most patients, they are granted high social status, and they have tremendous political influence. By contrast, patients are sick, scared, and in pain; and they have been well socialized into a subservient position. Because genuine informed consent assumes little to no coercion, and because the noted power asymmetry is inherently coercive, such valid consent is rarely achieved, and thus patient autonomy is routinely undercut.

Power asymmetry is inherently
coercive [and] patient autonomy
is routinely undercut

Furthermore, because decisions are, as per this argument, driven by physician values, or at best by physician understanding of patient values, patients are often directly harmed. They may receive inappropriate medical procedures and be treated beyond the point of real value, often with considerable consequent pain and degradation, because such treatment satisfies an array of physician and hospital interests.

Similar analyses have been made of lawyer–client relationships.[4] The concern is, again, whether the distinct power asymmetry between attorney and client results in the latter's autonomy being threatened or welfare damaged. Wasserstrom (1988) concluded that it does: "The relationship between the lawyer and the client is typically, if not inevitably, a morally defective one in which the client is not treated with the respect and dignity he or she deserves" (p. 65). As with medicine, the asymmetry is rooted in lawyers' specialized knowledge, technical language, and social status, combined with clients' vulnerability due to what they typically have at stake in legal proceedings—their liberty, their property, even their life. These differences "conspire to depersonalize the client in the eyes of the professional" (p. 67).

We grant that there are important differences between these relationships and those that typically exist between journalists and their subjects and sources. In medicine and law, roles are more clearly established, the patient or client has typically sought the help of the physician or lawyer, the specialized knowledge gap is wide, and there is a clear social assignment of prestige. Such asymmetries are also present in journalist–subject/source relationships, but rarely are they as distinct. In fact, it is because they are not, because there is not a clearly defined professional–client relationship, that many have concluded that journalism does not qualify as a profession.[5]

Despite these differences, however, we believe there is enough similarity to make a like analysis cogent; indeed, there is reason to believe the problem may be even more acute in journalistic relationships. The essential foundation of most professional relationships is client benefit, or at least mutual benefit. The very purpose is to enhance the client's health, to help her manage the legal system, to assist in her learning or spiritual growth, and so forth. Although we acknowledge these beneficial goals are not always achieved, that not all professional relationships match their avowed purpose, mostly they are. They do because the purpose is so avowed, and because our system is designed to also benefit the professional (compensation, social respect, prestige, etc.) when client benefit is achieved.

> *The journalistic relationship*
> *seems fundamentally to be ...*
> *grounded in each party's desire*
> *to satisfy his or her respective*
> *self-interest.*

In journalistic relationships there also can be mutual benefit—the journalist wants a good story, and the subject or source wants to be presented in a good light or have her ideas widely and accurately disseminated. But, such benefit is not essential to the interaction. Rather, the reality is probably closer to Ralph Barney's somewhat pessimistic assessment that, "Every interview is a power struggle."[6] That is, the journalistic relationship seems fundamentally to be, if not Barney's antagonism, at least grounded in each party's desire to satisfy his or her respective self-interest, but also being more or less wary of the other. Each may wish to remain in the other's good graces and may even genuinely care about the other's well being, but neither such goal is fundamental to the relationship, as it is in effective health care, legal assistance, teaching, ministry, and so forth.

Hence, who holds the power in these interactions is critical. Our conclusion is that it is usually the reporter. Recall the definition of power—the ability to achieve one's agenda, usually by manipulating others. Granting certain exceptions, which I will discuss, agenda control clearly rests in the hands of the journalist. The journalist decides what stories to cover, how to cover them, how to characterize the various people and ideas, and so forth. Although some norms dictate appropriate choices here, they are *institutional* norms, chosen by journalists, not by subjects and sources. Thus, determining what is newsworthy, let alone how it will be portrayed, lies in the hands of the journalist.

Power is then reinforced through the interview process. The reporter establishes what the story is about, arranges the interview, asks the questions, interrupts at her discretion, and determines the pace of the conversation.[7] Furthermore, just as physicians and lawyers have their trappings of power (white coats, stethoscopes, three-piece suits, elevated judge plat-forms), so also do reporters: the ubiquitous notepad and badges for print, camera equipment and attire for TV. Because they have become a standard part of the journalist's daily life, she may no longer even be aware of their presence. The even minimally cognizant subject or source, however, is acutely aware of them and of the power they represent.

Finally, and most important, is who controls the outcome. Journalists hold near complete control over what happens to a story: They edit it at their discretion, thereby giving it their spin. Their editors or producers de-termine whether it will run and, if so, with what kind of play. Of course, it is also their printing press or television station. The cliché is now treated as a joke, but it is nonetheless accurately revealing of who holds the power in these relationships: Never pick a fight with someone who buys ink by the barrel.

Consider the neophyte subject or source. He is initially flattered to be in-terviewed, to be either identified as a relevant expert or to be considered worthy of news interest. This creates an immediate asymmetry of grati-tude. He, furthermore, lacks skills in managing the interview to make sure his interests are heard and understood. He is not media-savvy in creating sound bites or catchy quotes. He does not know how to spark the re-porter's interest in his concerns, so he will have a better chance of having his ideas correctly conveyed. He simply answers questions and, having lit-tle other choice, places his trust in the reporter. Unfortunately, perhaps more often than not, he turns on the evening news or picks up the morning paper, lets out a curse and mutters, "That's not what I said, or at least it's not what I meant!"

> *Persons in positions of authority*
> *… typically succeed in reversing*
> *the power asymmetry.*

Even the experienced subject or source is still out of the journalist's league. When we presented these ideas at the PEEC Colloquium (see note 6), Lee Wilkins pulled one of us aside to argue that persons in positions of authority (political, social, economic) typically succeed in reversing the power asymmetry. Authoritative subjects and sources, she argued, control the interview process because the journalist is so beholden to them for in-formation. Wilkins' point is well taken, but in an important sense such au-thoritative persons are the exception that proves the rule, because so few subjects and sources are in a position to make the journalist dependent on them. The vast majority, even those with the experience-based knowledge and skills needed to better manage interviews, realize, ultimately, the story is defined by the journalist.[8] The journalist still controls whether the story will run, what it will say, and how the subject or source will be portrayed. In short, the journalist still controls the printing press and the airwaves.

Thus, ironically, the very enterprise that is supposed to enhance citizens' autonomy at the same time effectively undermines the autonomy of subjects and sources. It does so by having the power to control the agenda and, thus, to thwart, or at least to lessen, subjects' and sources' ability to make and act upon choices consistent with their life plan and character. Further, the asymmetry also brings great potential for other sorts of moral harm. Subjects and sources can be embarrassed, have their reputations destroyed, have their privacy violated, lose any chance for achievement of political or economic goals, and so forth. In short, the ethical implications of the asymmetry are significant.

Thus, we have two suggestions for how to mitigate these potential harms. First, journalism should more fully embrace its position as a profession. This will result in an inclusion of respect for subjects and sources as part of its fundamental purpose. Thus, even when a potentially harmful story is deemed important enough to run, there will be a concomitant emphasis on mitigating those harms, one as strong as the commitment to getting the story, or at least nearly so. Second, and related, this shift in fundamental purpose should also produce a change in the cultural ethos. Journalists currently take a certain pride in being curmudgeonly, even to the point of being rude and abusive. Seeing, instead, subjects and sources as persons about whom they must show concern, as worthy of being granted dignity and respect, can only serve to lessen harm. The Society of Professional Journalists' Code of Ethics is a good starting point for some of these concerns, especially the section on Minimizing Harm. The Code, though, does not acknowledge the sorts of power asymmetries discussed here; hence if journalists are going to take concomitant harms seriously, they will need to go beyond its rather limited recommendations.

These changes also would have an important impact on journalism's status as an institution. Let us, thus, now turn to those concerns.

Power at Institutional or Professional Level

We are not hapless beings caught in the grip of forces we can do little about, and wholesale damnations of our society only lend a further mystique to organization. Organization has been made by man; it can be changed by man. It has not been the immutable course of history that has produced such constrictions on the individual as personality tests. It is organization man who has brought them to pass and it is he who can stop them. (Whyte, 1956, p. 13)

As we have just seen, the instrumental use of power can be effectively understood at the individual level. Using this lens, interviews, clinical appointments, and legal consultations all become interpersonal encounters with more or less concrete agendas, usually facilitated by an inequitable distribution of power. Ethics, then, remedies this situation by emerging as a means for redistributing power among the participants, and/or advocating responsible use of authority. As we move to broader social levels, however, power's face and function are more complex. Although these dynamics inform the interpersonal (e.g., doctors' power is societally conferred and legitimated), it is important to explore the intricacies of institutional power in their own right. The institutional level is the key site where the personal meets the social, as these institutions come to embody the values of the people who inhabit them.

In Whyte's (1956) critique of Corporate America and its concomitant Social Ethic, he lamented the person who identifies with the organization to such a degree that he or she absorbs its institutional culture and even takes his or her identity from it. This person has become the organization or, by extension, profession, and as such, has been asked to consciously or unwittingly subscribe to its deepest core values, performing according to procedures it dictates. Whyte explained that these individuals, "tend to assume that the ends of organization and morality coincide, and on such matters as social welfare they give their proxy to the organization" (p. 8). It is important to remember that under Western ethical systems, people are taught to think of ethics in terms of individual responsibility, individual accountability, individual culpability, and individual moral decision making, fueled by an emphasis on individual autonomy and rationality. One result of all this individuation is, however, the obfuscation of how power actually functions as a moral force in organizations. Charles Taylor (1995) noted that proceduralism often underlies this veneer, writing that

> if the right thing to do has still to be understood as what is rationally justifiable, then the justification has to be procedural. It cannot be defined by the particular outcome but by the way in which the outcome is arrived at. (p. 148)

Proceduralism ... becomes an obstacle to the exercise of individual ethics rather than its guarantor.

This proceduralism is evident in all our institutions and organizations, most obviously law, but also medicine, where the procedure is trusted to produce a moral outcome. Certainly journalism is no exception, because it is a profession where practitioners take considerable training in the methods for gathering a story, and defend those methods as producing ethically sound stories. But, procedures are constrained by the imperfections, incompleteness or investments of not only those who shaped these procedures but, more profoundly, by their fundamental nature. Here we will examine three of proceduralism's dominant qualities: anonymity, institutionalization, and routinization, and their consequences as they interlocute with power, and what that means for journalistic ethics. We will see how proceduralism, then, becomes an obstacle to the exercise of individual ethics rather than its guarantor.

Proceduralism Is Anonymous

Ethics do not have a face, because ethics are often practiced as a disembodied set of guidelines, codes or rules that anyone can follow, and everyone should or must follow. Most professions and organizations try to establish rules they believe will ensure uniform ethical conduct. If the rules are right, then justice can exist "in a nation of devils," as Kant would say. An individual's value is as a member of a system. The danger to this kind of professional morality is illustrated in Hariman's (1995) discussion of bureaucratic style and the relationship between what he termed *decorum*, which he defined as an embodiment of a cultural ethic, and power. Here members of an organization or profession become bound to a way of performing their work identity. As workers fulfill their responsibilities, they often unwittingly become the role the institution has set for them. Power relationships become embedded in the structure of this performance of an organizational or professional identity, and the values that drive the procedures are subsumed in the behaviors expected. In journalism, rarely is there an opportunity to explore or question the rich moral texture of the values that drive the profession. When journalists have the opportunity to think of ethics at all, they have been encouraged to think about codes, rules, procedures, and action-oriented outcomes, and to rely on the moral excellence of ethical protocols rather than explore professional values. For example, most professional journalistic organizations have codes for their members to follow, and most professional literature examines appropriate courses of action. Emphasis in journalism ethics on prescribed courses of action and institutional or professional guidelines for newsgathering encourages a problematic, disengaged performance of the journalist's role when justification for moral responsibility is required.

The ethical fruit of this faceless anonymity is a lack of tangible accountability. The codes and canons follow a detached system of ethics that is connected neither to the context nor to the specific outcome. Such an environment sanitizes individuals from moral responsibility. Instead of individual members of an organization or profession taking responsibility for their decisions, there is always the procedure that can absorb the moral responsibility. Thus, people are shielded from authentic moral agency. No more chilling account of the results of this kind of culture can be found than Lifton's (1986) work on Nazi doctors. Lifton found that early accounts of the Holocaust death camps could not account for the behavior of all the people who participated in this slaughter. Rather, framing the executions as a procedure meant that each person doing some act of cruelty was only one step in a larger chain of murder. Killing became faceless by blaming the procedure for any moral wrongdoing, but individuals were safely hidden behind the inhuman walls of its protection.

Although journalists are hardly on parallel with death camp workers, the basic tenet is illustrative of the mechanism for removing accountability when people rely heavily on institutionally embedded and sanctioned practices. One general example of this kind of facelessness in journalism can be seen in the general prohibition against apologizing for the content of their stories or their consequences, but only for the procedure used in gathering the story. In fact, Daniel Schorr (personal communication, May 23, 1994) once observed that it is a journalist's responsibility to tell the truth, with no regard for the consequences. Another journalist, who requested anonymity in return for the interview, said, "It just comes with the territory. Sometimes people kill themselves" (personal communication, June 27, 1996). He wasn't trying to be callous, but merely to indicate that the consequences of a story are not his responsibility, provided he has fulfilled his professional obligations in gathering the story. Once the ethics guiding a profession become faceless, individuals no longer feel obligated to take personal responsibility for the stories they produce.

Proceduralism Is Institutional

Proceduralism is also shaped by the internal mechanisms and structures of its host organization and institution. In America, a primary value is efficiency. Early in the 20th century, Frederick Taylor (1947) and his cadre of efficiency experts sought to create efficient workers by scientifically managing the mechanics of performing work routines. The end result was not only to increase profits, as Taylor projected, but to dehumanize the American worker, whose thinking was separated from physical labor by design. This organizational value soon permeated American culture and the expectations for every institution and organization from fast food to higher education. The key to efficiency, Taylor found, was standardization, with procedure the fundamental means by which to accomplish it.

The work of organizational culture scholars (e.g., Pacanowsky & O'Donnell-Trujillo, 1983), revealed that organizations inculcate their cultural values through rituals, narrative, and performative interactions, such as learning and teaching roles and "ropes" (as in "learning the ..."). Journalism is no different; organizations instill professional values this same way (Darnton, 1975). With deadline pressures of modern journalism, gathering information in the most efficient manner is a premium skill (as most basic reporting texts will indicate). In an ironic abuse of this ethos, one of the excuses *New York Times* reporter Jayson Blair gave for plagiarizing stories and inventing facts was the pressure to produce quickly. Moreover, the very form of news embodies efficiency. Sound bites and *USA Today* aside, the traditional news form of the inverted pyramid and its variations is designed to communicate as much information in as short a time as possible.

> *Efficiency and standardization induce static, monolithic moral decision-making.*

The qualities of efficiency and standardization induce static, monolithic moral decision-making. Once institutional or professional procedures for dealing with particular moral problems are in place, those within the institution rely on them as trustworthy and even convenient means of avoiding the personal and professional crises of conscience potential in analyzing every case. Not only would such introspection be inefficient, and thus violate the goals of the organization, but it would also undermine the moral authority of the institution. In fact, many scholars have begun to see proceduralism as the moral template thwarting ethical dialogue and change (Sandel, 1996; Sunstein, 1993; Taylor, 1995). A recent article dealing with coverage of suicide (Miller, 2002) detailed various major papers' guidelines for what content to include with respect to this thorny issue.

What most seemed to take for granted is that codes of newsworthiness drive the news organization to do some sort of story. Newsworthiness itself is a value of the profession, and as it is institutionalized, journalists find it increasingly difficult to challenge. Yet, most journalists interviewed noted that stories such as those about suicides are so contextual and sensitive that guidelines are virtually useless. In these cases, the dictates of efficiency and speed then guide newsgathering and reporting.

Veblen (1899, 1904) illustrated how the power of proceduralism thwarts change. He claimed that when people are trained in a set of procedures, they find it virtually impossible to adapt to a shift in environment. He called such people *institutional men,* and cited prisoners so accustomed to one way of doing things in the penal system that they cannot adapt to the freedom or environmental changes of the outside world.

> *The [penal system] analogy does*
> *serve to illustrate the stultifying*
> *influence of procedure*
> *to contextual sensitivity*
> *and adaptation.*

Although people who work in the professions or in specific organizations are hardly prisoners, the analogy does serve to illustrate the stultifying influence of procedure to contextual sensitivity and adaptation. Especially in the case of the news media, whose usual rationale for resisting formal ethical regulation is "every case is different," contextual sensitivity and the appreciation for moral complexity and adaptability are key components in negotiating their ethical terrain. Although they need not degenerate into the relativism that "every case is different" implies, it is an understandable professional reaction to the constraints and ultimately ethically unsatisfying moral choices that the proceduralism inherent in their craft demands. The ultimate outcome of this efficiency focus is that individuals become mindless and are no longer compelled to reflect on the discourse they produce.

Proceduralism Is Routine

One final quality of an institution is its ability to move toward a set of goals that are viewed as a means for ensuring objectivity. Thus, procedures serve to routinize and normalize the everyday operations of the organization or institution and, theoretically, eliminate the political bias found in the broader community. Most organizations and professions—even those who, by definition, deal in contingencies, such as medicine or journalism—create and arrange a set of daily activities that establishes the rhythm of the workday. Routinizing work in this way creates security against the unpredictable or different, and thus produces a feeling of normalcy. The tacit routines themselves reinforce and thus substitute for what is accepted as morally right. Ritzer's (1996, 2001) McDonaldization studies contended that American institutions have set up a relationship between an ethical code of efficiency, predictability, and mechanization and the expectations of the American public. Organizations are the modern factory, establishing internal procedures that, once routinized, mask the power inherent in these organizations to dictate value structures to the larger society.

Within journalism specifically, Tuchman's (1972) studies of the sociology of the newsroom furnished early examples of how objectivity, routinized as a newsgathering methodology, reifies a moral expectation that actually serves to obviate ethical responsibility, as well as to institutionalize a defining ethos for the profession. Tuchman (1973) also explored how journalists routinize the unexpected. Other studies have examined, for example, how coverage of airline crashes and natural disasters has been proceduralized, and in so doing, function to reinforce certain societal and professional norms (Vincent, Crow, & Davis, 1989), as well as how news organizations normalize conflict, even in their own newsrooms (Bantz, 1985). The central insight of these studies is that exceptional events are treated with little creativity and, thus, the means for reporting them begin to shape the ways they are reported.

> *If power is invisible, it is impossible to manage its morality, counter its consequence, or redistribute it more fairly.*

When procedures that transform the work environment into a set of taken-for-granted routines performed in almost unconscious fashion are firmly established in the organization, power becomes invisible. Cloaked in the mundane realities of executing a task, power is free to exercise itself on behalf of the value structure that drives it. If power is invisible, it is impossible to manage its morality, counter its consequences, or redistribute it more fairly. Further, its role in the ethical process is masked as well, making it far more difficult to resolve intractable ethical tensions. Foucault (1965) considered the damaging effects of normalizing medical treatments to the moral integrity of the medical profession. He recounted how historically the mentally ill were dominated through a set of procedures based on Enlightenment ideals such as control, categorization, scientific method, and the impulse to know and manage the world. Although we would look at some of these procedures as cruel by modern standards, or simply ridiculous and feckless, Foucault noted that no one questioned the power of the medical establishment to say what constitutes illness, or to pronounce someone cured. Even now the medical profession has a great deal of power over the body, power masked by the legitimacy of the institution.

Applying a discussion of invisibility to the news media has great significance for media ethics. Although the media themselves have steadily lost credibility as authoritative, many scholars have noted that they still effectively perpetuate the authority and credibility of other social institutions, themselves bureaucratized and suffering from the ethical pitfalls of proceduralism. Moreover, journalism itself has proceduralized ethical decision making, where it is considered at all, and thus cloaks the power behind its own set of unquestioned values, foisted on the American or Western public, and even the global community—one way journalists exercise their own form of invisible power in framing news stories. Coleman's (1995) examination of coverage surrounding an environmental controversy revealed how use of specific sources served to frame the story to ideologically privilege the scientific perspective. Thus, everyday journalistic methods can impact their objectivity in such ways that objectivity itself becomes a mask for institutional bias.

To the extent that proceduralism shuts off ethical sensibilities, and veils the influence that power wields in journalistic moral decision making, it is a destructive force in professional ethics. It is important to remember that although an institution can create an ethical climate, it cannot ensure an ethical outcome through mere rules. Reliance on procedurally derived norms leads to a model of the moral self that is atavistic, atomistic, removed from the social, and ultimately irresponsible. Although it seemingly creates a culture of equality by promoting fairness and agency, and part of its strong appeal certainly stems from the alluring promise that everyone participates under a procedure equally, proceduralism both encourages and assumes disconnection from the community.

Ironically, and unfortunately, proceduralism undercuts the kind of society it promises to create by eliminating individual responsibility. As Sandel (1996) contended, good government (and, by extension, a good society supported by good professions) relies on citizens who have a "moral bond with the community whose fate is at stake" (p. 5). The journalistic community, and professions generally, are marked precisely by a detachment from the community whose fate is at stake. Even in the case of law, legal advocates are, by nature, part of a legal system fundamentally premised on impartiality, detachment, and faith in a procedure to yield justice, rather than on the integrity of any individuals within it.[9] Certainly in the case of journalism, it is a common assumption that the quality of the craft is predicated on detachment, and the character of individual journalists should not matter, provided they follow the same set of procedures for newsgathering. In this way, proceduralism actually can undo the noble ethical goal of social justice, by removing the individual from the moral calculus. For journalism in particular, and professions generally, to make moral headway against the seemingly persistent ethical dilemmas that face them, and to produce reflective practitioners whose vocation is ethically satisfying in the whole of their lives, they must challenge the dominant framework for viewing their moral task, despite the fact that media organizations do not want to acknowledge these power structures, much less discuss them.

Proceduralism will not yield easily for, as we have seen, not only does it have a partnership with power, but has become our Western, secular religion, thus pitting it against other global systems of thought and social forces, which we will examine in the following.

Power at Global or Macrolevel

We contend that it is a matter of epistemological necessity to examine the connection between power and ethics. Thus, this section deals with the concept of power as an operational and theoretical concept in the journalistic enterprise. We examine this issue at a macro-level, having explored earlier how power can be contextualized at the individual and the institutional levels. Focusing on journalism as practiced in the West we draw from adjacent fields of knowledge, and particularly from a distinctly postcolonial thought, that is imperative to the understanding of the location of power in the inquiry of ethics. What follows, then, is the discussion of the nature of power, the motives of power, the location of power and the cultural context of journalists in this location of power—all of which have a bearing on the practice and scholarship of professional ethics.

Ethics of mass media, like many other professional arenas, at a broad level, are constantly in a flux (Babbili, 1997). Far from being a constant, the very idea of ethics is being shaped and reshaped in a turbulent global arena in which conflicting and contending systems of thought, social forces, and ideologies collide and collude on the precise nature of morality and moral conduct. Postcolonial thought, that focuses on the consequences of power relations at both the micro and macro-levels, forces one to examine critically the concept of power—placing it in the domain of professional, institutional, and global practices (Breckenridge & Van Der Veer, 1994; Prakash, 1995).

Media ethics as a field of inquiry cannot be detached from its global and competing ideologies and narratives.

Amidst the never-ending struggle between dominant ideologies at an international level, power has come to occupy, or ought to occupy, a central place in the study of professional ethics (Bottomore, 1979; Burchill, Linklater, Devetak, Peterson, & True, 1996). Power has been analyzed earlier at micro and institutional levels in this essay. Before we examine the idea of power at a macro level and the context of journalism as a profession, it has to be noted that media ethics as a field of inquiry cannot be detached from its global and competing ideologies and narratives. Professional ethics and morality are in fundamental tension, because they are arguably rooted in their respective idiosyncratic and diasporic cultures (Christians & Traber, 1997). Power is the single most important crucial aspect that has the capacity to reveal the true nature of social forces that both undermine and underpin the study of what is right or wrong in professional conduct.

Understanding the working definitions of power, as an operating concept at the macro level, calls for the tolerance of interdisciplinarity (Babbili, 1990). They stem from a broad spectrum of academic fields, notably from fields such as political sociology (Bottomore, 1979), international relations and political theory (Walker, 1993), cultural studies (Blundell, Shepherd, & Taylor, 1993; Hall, 1980), feminist theory (Skeggs, 1995), studies in imperialism (Cheyfitz, 1991; Morgenthau, 1967; Said, 1993), and most challenging, from postcolonial theory (Prakash, 1995). Consequently, power, here, is defined as the ability of a professional organization, an institution, a nation-state, or a group of nations, a society or cultural entity to pursue or maintain a course of action (to make and implement decisions, and more broadly, to determine the agenda for decision making), if necessary, against the interests and even against the opposition of other organizations, institutions, nation-states, or cultural groups (Bottomore, 1979).

Diverse conceptualizations of power can be found within particular theories of society and politics. The notion of power may also include such cognate notions of authority and influence that are used in various theoretical schemes as we have seen earlier in this article.

Relevant to the study of professional ethics, power can be located in the social and cultural aspects of human communication. Consequently, journalism and communication can be located in the conduct of international power relations, in cultural and religious thought and practice, in the maintenance of status quo, in imperial habit (imperialism), in hegemony of colonial thought, and in professional ethics. Power manifests itself when the journalist, as a professional immersed in a professional ideology, operates from a position of power; and when the journalist himself or herself becomes an agent and extension of this power. One must perceive the professional journalist as immersed in the power of ideology of a particular institution and culture that he or she represents. Journalists should also be seen as extensions of such power in the exercise of their role, function, and professional ethos. We contend that the power professional journalists represent is less apparent to the journalist than to news consumers.

Journalism, thus, is not merely local or national; it is global and international. What we do in journalism and media ethics has a bearing on the global community of professional journalists (Babbili, 1997). How do we compromise journalism ethics embedded in the United States culture and society or of the West, in general, with the practice of journalism worldwide and with global realities that are in a constant flux (Golding & Harris, 1997)?

That international communication (particularly, journalism) plays a crucial role in maintaining power relations between countries or regions becomes evident when we study the nature of 20th century politics (Morgenthau, 1967; Schuman, 1969). Power in international politics in the first half of the 20th century raised for the professional journalist problems of unprecedented difficulty and seriousness. The state system that rose from the ruins of medieval power bore three characteristics: a balance of power composed of a multiplicity of European nations of more or less equal strength, of which Great Britain (and the United States?) were strong and detached enough to maintain that balance; a shared set of moral values that guided the Western world in their relations with each other; and, essentially stationary technology which supported only limited warfare.

However, by the middle to latter part of the century, international politics went through a power balance pitting the United States and the Western world against the Soviet Union and the socialist bloc. Nevertheless, by the 1990's, the predictable scenario of the traditional balance of power had disintegrated with the United States emerging as an undisputed global and military power. This was accompanied by a fierce struggle in the postcolonial world, whereby many nations formerly ruled or exploited by Western nations gained independence, sometimes, amidst chaos, imposition of dictatorships and/or theocracies, and other undemocratic systems of power.

Professional journalistic ideologies triggered by these events and changes, and accompanied by an explosion in innovative communication technologies, has resulted in the rise of undisputed dominance of Western media corporations and news cartels.

This global media landscape is highlighted by such controlling corporations as Viacom, AOL/Time Warner, NewsCorp., Walt Disney, Bertlesmann, Vivendi/Universal and so on over news and information. Even the largest news agencies, Associated Press, Havas-AFP, Reuters, United Press International, and others, belong to stockholders primarily of the West. Moreover, journalists who work for these corporations, whether in a news gathering enterprise or in an image making capacity, remain stakeholders in these corporations. (Altschull, 1984; Herman & McChesney, 1997). Herein lies the dilemma of how media and political ideologies can be studied in the context of power manifesting itself in these emerging global realities.

Various motives of power in international relations are relevant to the study of power in journalistic conduct.

It can be argued that various motives of power use in international relations are relevant to the study of power in journalistic conduct. A primary use of power is to maintain the status quo in international relations. By status quo, we mean continued dominance of West over East, the technologically advanced over the agrarian. Increasing consolidation of media conglomerates can be seen as a solidifying force in the maintenance of such status quo in power relations. Another power use is expansion—whether imperial or institutional. Both journalism and international relations reflect the tendency to impose professional ideologies to expand and influence. The other motive of power is to gain prestige or indisputable legitimacy. Journalistic professionalism of the West, again, can be seen as an extension of such an ideology. More importantly, a crucial motive of the powerful is to advance dominant cultural narratives that speak to the supremacy of West over East. Coverage of international events, crises, and wars, analyses of these events, a particular worldview on global realities, images of virtue and vice emanate from the channels of western media organizations. These images gain currency around the world courtesy of powerful news organizations such as CNN, the BBC, Sky TV, and other Western organizations. This advancing of a dominant cultural narrative has several operational methods: ideological, institutional, cultural, and so forth, which effectively encase ideas of authority and influence (MacKenzie, 1995; Said, 1978; Sharafuddin, 1994).

The power of journalism, thus, cannot be decontextualized from the power of the dominant Western ideology, in which Western media conglomerates play active and aggressive roles. The hegemonic influence the Western media exert on non-Western cultures and nations is largely exercised by the global news cartel. Here we can invoke Edward Said's (1978) seminal critique of the Orientalist discourses in the Western news media.

Through Said (1978) we see the power of Western academic and journalistic enterprise in constructing texts of other cultures while creating a geopolitical awareness among the Western audiences. Journalistic power can be further seen, within this Orientalist critique, in a deeply rooted and self-serving bias, and in its ability to elaborate on and perpetuate the basic historical and geographical distinctions, that is, East versus West, Orient versus the Occident, modern versus traditional, historical versus ahistorical, advanced versus impoverished, and so on. Western journalism paints images of the East based on what the West wants to see there. These images nurture the taproot of the colonial imagination perpetrated by several centuries of travel writing and international reporting. Said also articulated the power of Western journalism and literature, and other communication media, as the primary marketing agents of a distinctly Anglo-Saxon worldview. The very fabric of imagination the Western people possess is based on the ability of the media to sketch an imagery that utilizes an established lexicon and vocabularies of Western dominance. This power of journalism in the last two centuries, especially, has resulted in a Western hegemony of ideas and images and in a dominant ideology presented skillfully and disarmingly through its cultural narratives.

> *The fabric of Western*
> *imagination is based*
> *on … imagery that utilizes*
> *an established lexicon*
> *and vocabularies of*
> *Western dominance.*

Uniquely, the study of postcolonial discourses finds theoretical support for its critique of this Western journalistic enterprise in Said. Postcolonialism, in a broader sense, sees Western global journalism as steeped in bipolar vocabularies and images. For example, Europe and the West are advanced through the journalistic enterprise as rational, virtuous, mature and, normal. The Orient, on the other hand, is advanced as irrational, depraved, childlike and different. Oddly enough, Said's exposition found a strange bedfellow in Walter Lippmann (1922). Lippmann's set of arguments, published just after World War I, mirrored some of Said's main contentions on the power and ability of Western communications enterprise to advance a particular ideology of dominance. Lippmann, in a psycho-sociological sense, lamented in the early 1900s the schism between the "world outside and the pictures in our heads" (p. 3). Lippmann's concerns included the inaccurate and incomplete portrayals of international realities in the news media. The news media of the West erect images of the Eastern realities through the perpetuation of stereotypes that result in a lopsided superficiality. Here again, Lippmann referred to a limited vocabulary journalists use in the imaging of things non-Western and in the construction of complex realities at a macrolevel.

Even today, the traditional news values in the powerful enterprise of Western news reporting is based on values that determine the sheer newsworthiness of non-Western realities: national interest, military relations, economic ties, historical alliances, and cultural proximity. In the prism of Western news, the Western journalist sees the events in the global arena essentially through the dictates of the stated or perceived national (and, by extension, corporate) interest. The nations that have military relations with the United States, such as the countries of NATO, are deemed to be more newsworthy than others. Economically, too, countries that have a clear financial interest or trade ties with the United States are perceived to be most important. Too, countries with established historical links to the United States tend to be of more relevance or consequence. Cultural proximity as a news value implies that those countries sharing distinct history, religion, or customs (i.e. an Anglo-Saxon foundation, a Judeo-Christian ideology and so on) have a favored view compare to that of the rest of the world.

Power relationships (journalist–subject, journalist–audience and so on) must be contextualized within culture, ideology, and religions, because construction of images, in reality, are dictated by self-defined ethical constraints emanating from such factors.

Let us take religions, for a brief example. In a postcolonial construct, major religions of the world can be categorized as expansionist and nonexpansionist. Religions that are expansionist in nature inherently possess a spiritual mandate to spread these religions around the world. In such a category belong Christianity and Islam. Hinduism and Judaism represent the nonexpansionist category of religions. Varying definitions of power across religions and cultures and across the ideological spectrum of journalistic professionalism call for an understanding of the conditions in which journalists operate. Religio-cultural factors may impinge more on, say, journalists in Islamic societies than in the Judeo-Christian countries. In the same vein, postcolonial societies, like that of India and of the British Commonwealth, may place a premium on operational values of journalism, in morality and moral practice that are seemingly contradictory. Journalism in nondemocratic countries may lend itself to varying definitions of power relative to that of the democratic world.

Similarly, the power of journalism, through the prisms of religion and culture, has varying degrees of influence and authority in the developing countries. Journalistic professionalism seen through the lens of Islam and of Hinduism reflects power and influence of the media over the masses it purports to serve just as much as the profit-driven news media in a capitalistic milieu. The study of media ethics, thus, must reflect such obvious underpinnings stemming from social and cultural ideologies (Christians & Traber, 1997). For journalism and power are inherent in a cultural ethos in which the journalist operates. The study of media ethics must eschew the traditional notions of morality and moral practices of the West and broaden the scope of such studies to include culture, ideology, and religions of the East. One can only do so by studying the idea of power that exerts itself in international journalism—communication at a macrolevel.

Conclusion

Contrary to what seemed to be so at the outset, there is an integrative pattern that emerges out of the examination of power at the individual, institutional, and global and comparative levels of the study of media ethics. We have attempted here to demonstrate the link between power and the journalistic practice. The relationship between power and the practicing journalist, between power and the institutions of mass media, and between power and the West's global journalistic enterprise is supported by streams of direct, indirect, and conflicting evidence. Yet, to our knowledge, scholars have seldom attempted to create a strong and potent theoretical link between them. In its broadest sense, then, this article represents the beginning of a theoretical exegesis linking the field of media ethics with the idea of power. This task is, indeed, both a theoretical necessity as well as an intellectual imperative of our times.

Notes

1. See Russell (1986). Power is also sometimes understood as having control over nature. We think it is cleaner to think of such control as more skill or ability based, rather than as power per se. (We are grateful to Lisa Newton, Elliot Cohen, and Michael Davis for their helpful clarifications on this point.)
2. See Rawls (1999), especially pp. 450–456.
3. See Ainsworth-Vaughn (1998), Schneider (1998), Fisher (1983), and Waitzkin (1983), especially chapter 6, "The Micropolitics of the Doctor–Patient Relationship."
4. Richard Wasserstrom's article (1988) has become the standard here, reprinted in any number of legal and professional ethics texts. Similar analyses are also present in feminist legal theory (MacKinnon, 1993) and it is an underlying theme in many of the critiques of adversarialism (Applbaum, 1999).
5. See Ed Lambeth's (1992) succinct summary of the debate, pp. 106–108, and May (2001), pp. 196–204.
6. Comment at the PEEC Colloquium on Media Ethics, March 19, 2003, University of South Florida, St. Petersburg.
7. Linguists point to these kinds of markers as key to who holds power in conversations, using this sort of analysis as being a consistent structure underlying a range of different kinds of communication contexts. See Fisher (1983), Ainsworth-Vaughn (1998), and Tannen (2001).
8. As any number of people have pointed out in the aftermath of the Jayson Blair debacle, it is striking how few of his subjects and sources bothered to request a correction. It seems many simply saw it as part of the game—the journalist

holds the power and one just hopes one comes across well when the interview
finds its way into print. See Johnson (2003).

9. That is not to say that all attorneys lack moral integrity, despite the profession's humorous reputation for unscrupulous behavior. Nor is it to ignore or
discount the Bar Association's code of ethics, drawing some general boundaries for those who practice law. It is to say, however, that the legal system is
predominantly dependent on a set of procedures for everything from admissible evidence to jury selection. The jury and trial process is presumed to counterbalance human bias, present to some degree in even those of highest moral
character. And the hallmark of every profession has traditionally been objectivity, which of itself necessitates detachment.

References

Ainsworth-Vaughn, N. (1998). *Claiming power in doctor–patient talk.* New York: Oxford University Press.

Altschull, H. (1984). *Agents of power: The role of the news media in human affairs.* New York: Longman.

Applbaum, A. (1999). *Ethics for adversaries: The morality of roles in public and professional life.* Princeton, NJ: Princeton University Press.

Babbili, A. (1990). Understanding international discourse: Political realism and the non-aligned nations. *Media, Culture, and Society, 12,* 309–324.

Babbili, A. (1997). Ethics and the discourse on ethics in post-colonial India. In C. Christians & M. Traber (Eds.), *Communication ethics and universal values* (pp. 128–158). London: Sage.

Bantz, C. (1985). News organizations: Conflict as a crafted norm. *Communication, 8,* 225–244.

Blundell, V., Shepherd, J., & Taylor, I. (1993). *Relocating cultural studies: Developments in theory and research.* New York: Routledge.

Bottomore, T. (1979). *Political sociology.* New York: Harper & Row.

Breckenridge, C., & Van Der Veer, P. (Eds.). (1994). *Orientalism and the postcolonial predicament.* Philadelphia: University of Pennsylvania Press.

Burchill, S., Linklater, S., Devetak, A., Peterson, R., & True, M. (Eds.). (1996). *Theories of international relations.* New York: St. Martin's.

Cheyfitz, E. (1991). *The poetics of Imperialism: Translation and colonization from The Tempest to Tarzan.* New York: Oxford University Press.

Christians, C., & Traber, M. (1997). *Communication ethics and universal values.* London: Sage.

Coleman, C.-L. (1995). Science, technology, and risk coverage of a community conflict. *Media, Culture, and Society, 17,* 65–79.

Darnton, R. (1975). Writing news and telling stories. *Daedalus, 104,* 175–194.

Fisher, S. (1983). Doctor talk/patient talk: How treatment decisions are negotiated. In S. Fisher & A. Dundas Todd (Eds.), *The social interaction of doctor–patient communication* (pp. 135–158). Washington, DC: The Center for Applied Linguistics.

Foucault, M. (1965). *Madness and civilization: A history of insanity in the age of reason.* New York: Random House.

Golding, P., & Harris, P. (Eds.). (1997). *Beyond cultural imperialism: Globalization, communication and the New International Order*. London: Sage.

Hall, S. (1980). Cultural studies: Two paradigms. *Media, Culture, and Society, 2,* 57–72.

Hariman, R. (1995). *Political style: The artistry of power*. Chicago: University of Chicago Press.

Herman, E., & McChesney, R. (1997). *The global media: The new missionaries of corporate capitalism*. London: Cassell.

Johnson, R. (2003, June 6). Media must become introspective, experts say. *The Los Angeles Times*, p. A-29.

Lambeth, E. (1992). *Committed journalism: An ethic for the profession* (2nd ed.). Bloomington, IN: Indianapolis University Press.

Lifton, R. (1986). *The Nazi doctors: Medical killing and the psychology of genocide*. New York: Basic.

Lippmann, W. (1922). *Public opinion*. New York: Free Press.

MacKenzie, J. (1995). *Orientalism: History, theory, and the arts*. Manchester, England: Manchester University Press.

MacKinnon, K. (1993). Toward feminist jurisprudence. In P. Smith (Ed.), *Feminist jurisprudence* (pp. 610–619). New York: Oxford.

May, W. (2001). *Beleaguered rulers: The public obligation of the professional*. Louisville, KY: Westminster John Knox.

Miller, M. (2002, December). Tough calls: Deciding when a suicide is newsworthy and what details to include are among journalism's more sensitive decisions. *American Journalism Review*, pp. 42–47.

Morgenthau, H. (1967). *Politics among nations*. New York: Knopf.

Pacanowsky, M., & O'Donnell-Trujillo, N. (1983). Organizational communication as cultural performance. *Communication Monographs, 50,* 126–147.

Parsons, T. (1951). *The social system*. New York: Free Press.

Prakash, G. (1995). *After colonialism: Imperial histories and postcolonial displacements*. Princeton, NJ: Princeton University Press.

Rawls, J. (1999). *A theory of justice* (rev. ed.). Cambridge, MA: Belknap.

Ritzer, G. (1996). *The McDonaldization of society* (Rev. ed.). Thousand Oaks, CA: Pine Forge.

Ritzer, G. (2001*). Explorations in the sociology of consumption: Fast food, credit cards, and casinos*. Thousand Oaks, CA: Sage.

Russell, B. (1986).The forms of power. In S. Lukes (Ed.), *Power* (pp. 19–27). New York: New York University Press.

Said, E. (1993). *Culture and imperialism*. New York: Knopf/Random House.

Said, E. (1978). *Orientalism*. New York: Pantheon.

Sandel, M. (1996). *Democracy's discontent: America in search of a public philosophy*. Cambridge, MA: Belknap of Harvard University Press.

Schneider, C. (1998). *The practice of autonomy*. New York: Oxford University Press.

Schuman, F. (1969). *International politics*. New York: McGraw-Hill.

Sharafuddin, M. (1994). *Islam and romantic orientalism: Literary encounters with the Orient*. London: L. B. Tauris.

Skeggs, B. (1995). *Feminist cultural theory: Process and production.* Manchester, England: Manchester University Press.

Sunstein, C. (1993). *The partial constitution.* Cambridge, MA: Harvard University Press.

Tannen, D. (2001). *You just don't understand: Men and women in conversation.* New York: Quill.

Taylor, C. (1995). A most peculiar institution. In J. E. J. Altham & R. Harrison (Eds.), *World, mind, and ethics: Essays on the ethical philosophy of Bernard Williams* (pp. 132–155). Cambridge, England: Cambridge University Press.

Taylor, F. (1947). *Principles of scientific management.* New York: Harper & Row.

Tuchman, G. (1972). Objectivity as strategic ritual: An examination of newsmen's notions of objectivity. *American Journal of Sociology, 77,* 660–670.

Tuchman, G. (1973). Making news by doing work: Routinizing the unexpected. *American Journal of Sociology, 79*(1), 110–131.

Veblen, T. (1904). *The theory of business enterprise.* New York: Charles Scribner's Sons.

Veblen, T. (1964). *The theory of the leisure class: An economic study of institutions.* Reprinted, with an introduction by C. Wright Mills. London: Unwin. (Original work published 1899)

Vincent, R., Crow, B., & Davis, D. (1989). When technology fails: The drama of airline crashes in network television news. *Journalism Quarterly, 66,* 155–160.

Waitzkin, H. (1983). *The second sickness.* New York: The Free Press.

Walker, R. (1993). *Inside/outside international relations as political theory.* Cambridge, England: Cambridge University Press.

Wasserstrom, R. (1988). Lawyers as professionals: Some moral issues. In J. Callahan (Ed.), *Ethical issues in professional life* (pp. 58–69). New York: Oxford University Press.

Whyte, W., Jr. (1956). *The organization man.* New York: Simon & Schuster.

Journal of Mass Media Ethics, *19*(3&4), 247–275

Three Essays on Journalism and Virtue

G. Stuart Adam
Carleton University, Poynter Institute

Stephanie Craft
University of Missouri

Elliot D. Cohen
Indian River Community College

❏ *In these essays, we are concerned with virtue in journalism and the media but are mindful of the tension between the commercial foundations of publishing and broadcasting, on the one hand, and journalism's democratic obligations on the other. Adam outlines, first, a moral vision of journalism focusing on individualistic concepts of authorship and craft. Next, Craft attempts to bridge individual and organizational concerns by examining the obligations of organizations to the individuals working within them. Finally, Cohen discusses the importance of resisting the powerful corporate logic that pervades the news media in the United States and calls on journalists to be courageous.*

A Preface to the Ethics of Journalism
G. Stuart Adam

Politicians, professors, and members of the public routinely conflate the terms *media* and *journalism* when journalists and journalism are subjects of commentary and criticism. I regard this conflation as limiting. It makes the vision of journalism insufficiently precise, and it has the effect of burying ideas about the craft of journalism beneath the systems in which it is practiced. So I have separated the concept of journalism from that of media in this article, in the belief that discussions of ethical considerations associated with them both will be enriched. At the same time, I rely on and discuss the concepts of *authorship* and *craft* that are embedded in the concept of journalism. My goal is to provide what otherwise might be missed—namely, an understanding of the ethics of authorship or, more broadly, the ethics of discovery, representation, and analysis. That is why I am calling it A Preface.

The advantage of concentrating on craft is that it is possible to point directly, before brows furrow and utterances are made about the harm the media might do, to the moral foundations of journalism. In this respect, I am following what may be an old-fashioned approach inspired by, amongst others, John Gardner (1978), who believed of fiction, as I do of journalism, that it is (or mainly is) an art that strengthens politics and culture, and that there are a range of goods in it and arising out of it that we need urgently. We need to be reminded of these goods, lest we forget their value and become unduly cynical.

I hasten to add that by featuring journalism I am not saying the concept of media should be discarded. I accept that students of journalism, however much attention they should give to something called the ethics of craft and authorship, should be equally concerned with the ethics of media. In practical life, a journalist—as an editor or publisher rather than an independent writer—may be involved in the maintenance of systems and institutions and, thereby of media. It follows from this that his or her moral sense should be attuned to the venue and scope of such responsibilities. At the same time, I would like journalism students to understand first that the ethics of authorship call for a detailed and moral view of craft, and that is where I would like to begin. It is a matter of putting first things first.

So in what follows, I

- define journalism as a literary and moral craft,
- fold it into a democratic social contract,
- discuss the values driving the creation of its texts, and
- observe that a major source of our current concern is less with journalism and more with media.

> *Journalism comprises stories and commentary in the public media on events and ideas as they occur.*

On the last of these items, it may be said that television has enlarged the impulse in journalism to entertain rather than engage. It follows that citizens, news managers, network officials, owners and, above all, journalists themselves have a duty to bring that impulse under control and to ensure that journalism is concerned in a broad sense with governance and social understanding.

So what do we have in mind when we use the term journalism? In my view, journalism comprises stories and commentary in the public media on events and ideas as they occur (Adam, 1993). It is a form of expression, albeit media-based, just as the poem and novel are forms of expression. If poems are marked by a special syntax, rhythm, imagery, figures of speech, and rhyming, and novels are marked by fictions, chapters, characters, and long narratives, then journalism is marked by news, facts, narratives, and analyses. Further, although journalism is enriched by visual elements—sometimes by music in film and broadcasting—it is fundamentally literary. It is born in the act of writing—a text or even a cutline for publication or a script for broadcast—about things that happen in the here and now.

Lillian Ross (2002), formerly a writer for *The New Yorker*, made this point recently when she wrote in a series of meditations on her own work that journalism "is factual writing, and the highest kind of it comes in the form of good writing … . Every now and then," she said, "journalism has been found to be timeless; and its writers have been considered to be on a par with the best in literature" (p. 1). So Ross located journalism squarely in the domain of writing and literature. By emphasizing journalism's literary character, she diverted attention, at least for the moment, from the bureaucratic, managerial, and public policy concerns that rise on the head of the term media. She helped us to think initially of journalism as an outcome authorship.

It is important to note that she did this without sacrificing an understanding that journalism is also born in the identification of news and fact. She went on to say that she subscribed to the "who-what-when-where-why-and-how guidelines in journalism" (Ross, 2002, p. 1). In this respect, she shared a fundamental methodology with all journalists, including those concerned less with long narratives than hard news. But what she managed to do is take us from an exclusive preoccupation with the front page (and the lineup in news broadcasts), in which the collective efforts of journalists are the source of journalism's image, to the linguistic, analytical, and narrative lineaments—the DNA—of individual journalistic pieces, whether simple or complex.

So in the view I am promoting, journalists should be considered first as authors and the consideration of their ethical obligations should therefore be construed in relation to the activity of authorship and the creation of individual journalistic texts.

A Democratic Art

A second consideration of moral significance is that the authorship we are speaking of has evolved within a democratic system of government and a democratic civil society. In my view, journalism is a democratic art and the place and role of journalism is crucial to the operations of democracy.

I recognize as I say this that the meaning of the term *democracy* is not perfectly straightforward, largely because it is used as an abstraction and is thereby easily appropriated to political rhetoric by dictators as well as by democrats. Still, there are tests we can apply to determine if a society is genuinely democratic: Are there regular elections? Is citizenship inclusive and the franchise universal? Is there a stable constitution? Is there an independent judiciary? Are citizens free to form associations and gather in public places? Is speech free?

Positive answers to each of these questions incline us to a belief that our systems of government are democratic. I say "incline" because democracies are extremely complex structures, and I have not provided a comprehensive audit of all the practices that add up to it. However, it is a matter of moral relevance to note that a starting point for democratic life is freedom of speech. So writing in a democracy is an independent activity subject to very few, and precisely stated, legal rules; it follows, therefore, that the concept of freedom is embedded in the activity of journalism itself. The freedom to write is a foundation of democracy's architecture.

However, from the view of democratic theory, this is not the end of the matter. To the foregoing observations on freedom, one can add that those who constitute a free society have obligations to that society conferred on them through a social contract. Kymlicka (2002; interpreting Rawls and Dworkin) said the social contract should not be construed to mean a literal remembering of an original decision, made in a state of nature, to form a government. It is, by contrast, "a device for teasing out the implications of … moral premises concerning people's moral equality" (p. 61). In other words, incorporation of the concept of a social contract places journalists and their activities, however distant their work may be from the business of government, squarely in a citizenry of moral equals. Whatever else they might do or be, journalists collaborate with other citizens in the project of democratic government and the maintenance (and reform) of civil society and culture. So journalists as authors have duties as citizens to other citizens—to speak to them in their own language, to make wise news judgments, and to be empirical, forthright, honest, independent, eloquent, thoughtful, and reliable. As they discharge such moral obligations, they facilitate a democratic conversation, broadly considered.

However, that is not the end of this matter either. Democracy's processes, including journalism, are not (as some theorists imagine) natural or inevitable outcomes of such a contract—a simple product of freedom guided by a marketplace or hidden hand. They are the products of moral learning which are, or should be, embedded in the operations and methodology of the craft. Such a view is reflected in the words of Northrop Frye (1964) who said the following:

> Freedom has nothing to do with lack of training. You're not free to move unless you've learned to walk and not free to play the piano unless you practice.

Nobody is capable of free speech unless [he or she] learns how to use language, and such knowledge is not a gift; it has to be learned and worked at. (pp. 148–149)

Put differently, the operations of freedom are to be found in the disciplined application of clear standards that must be learned and worked at.

Reflection and Promoting Understanding

What do these standards entail? Stone (1988) summed the matter up nicely when he wrote:

The writer's responsibility ... consists in writing well and truly ... . The writer who betrays his calling is that writer who either for commercial or political reasons vulgarizes his own perception and rendering of it. [The author] assumes, above all, the responsibility to understand. (p. 75)

There are three components to Stone's formulation calling for reflection; one (to take the last first) having to do with understanding, another having to do with vulgarizing perceptions and beliefs, and the other having to do with the rendering of facts, perceptions, and beliefs so that they can be understood.

There is much that can be said about understanding. The protocols and methodology that journalists follow to set their work in motion are aimed at promoting understanding. Central to this process is reporting or, more broadly, evidence-gathering. In this respect, Kovach and Rosenstiel (2001) commented recently that journalism is a discipline of verification. "In the end," they wrote, "the discipline of verification is what separates journalism from entertainment, propaganda, [or] fiction" (p. 71). They went on to say that journalism alone "is focused on getting what happened down and right" (p. 71).

To endorse such a view of journalism requires recognition that facts matter, and that they can only be elicited through careful, and sometimes painstaking, research. But the operations of understanding involve more than research and the description of fact. They call for intellectual processes that include the identification of news and the description of its meaning and significance. Conferral of meaning results from a judgment not simply on the what and weight of certain verified facts, but on the objective connection between them. As a journalist composes a story, he or she studies the internal relations between facts to crystallize a news lead or *nut paragraph* (whether it is in the first paragraph or not). Sometimes the process goes wrong and there is, literally, a failure of understanding.

> *News judgments call for a*
> *commitment to truth that is as*
> *morally serious as the*
> *commitment to the facts on*
> *which they are constructed.*

Lyons (1994) provided a guide to such a failure in his critique of the series on the so-called Whitewater scandal that appeared in *The New York Times* in 1992. Lyons listed the errors made in the *Times'* investigative report and pointed, tellingly, to a claim made by reporters in rival organizations that, despite the richness of the alleged facts, the story "lacked a 'nut paragraph' summing up what the Clintons had done wrong and why it was important" (p. 56). Absence of such a paragraph was a signal that there was work still to be done or—this is hard to do after such an investment of time and labor—the text should have been discarded. So news judgments call for a commitment to truth that is as morally serious as the commitment to the facts on which they are constructed. The composition of a nut paragraph that is coherent and articulated to the facts is evidence that an intellectual process has led to understanding.

To say this is to direct attention again to the foundational importance of facts and the moral significance in journalism of sticking to them. Hersey (1986) addressed this matter eloquently when he wrote the following:

> I will assert that there is one sacred rule of journalism. The writer must not invent. The legend on the license must read: NONE OF THIS WAS MADE UP. The ethics of journalism … must be based on the simple truth that every journalist knows the difference between the distortion that comes from subtracting observed data and the distortion that comes from adding invented data. (p. 290)

So facts matter. In a manner of speaking, they are sacred. They are so sacred that at a minimum it is irritating, and at worst appalling, when journalists are careless with them. It is similarly disturbing when commercial or political forces intervene on the processes through which our world is brought to common consciousness through the exertions of journalists.

The risk of surrendering to such forces and vulgarizing beliefs, Stone's (1988) second category, called on the author to be courageous and, like a scientist, not allow ideology to trump experience. A telling example of how David Halberstam (1965) was tested in this respect is recorded in an essay he published titled "Getting the Story in Vietnam." The business of the essay included a description of how relations are routinely forged between diplomats and reporters on assignment in foreign lands. It went on to show how these relations operated during the Vietnam War and how, in due course, the views of Halberstam and his colleagues began to conflict with the views held and promoted by American diplomatic and military personnel. It was, one can tell, a painful experience for him. So he wrote:

> No one becomes a reporter to make friends, but neither is it pleasant in a situation like the war in Vietnam to find yourself so completely at odds with the views of the highest officials of your country. The pessimism of the Saigon press corps was of the most reluctant kind: many of us came to love Vietnam, we saw our friends dying all around us, and we would have liked nothing better than to believe the war was going well and that it would eventually be won. But it was impossible for us to believe those things without denying the evidence of our own senses … . And so we had no alternative but to report the truth. (p. 34)

Halberstam and his colleagues were forced by the facts to tell a bleeding nation that their officials were mistaken. So belief and judgment in journalism is subject to experience, as Halberstam (1965) said, to the evidence of our senses. Facts are sacred in journalism and democracies because experience, and its factual rendering, matters. From a writer's view, the language in which such facts are presented also matters in a moral sense.

Stone (1988) said the writer's responsibility consists in writing "well and truly"—a phrase Hemingway (1935) used in *Green Hills of Africa*. In the course of reflecting on the writer's experience of success, Hemingway said the experience is "something I cannot yet define completely, but the feeling comes when you write well and truly of something and you know impersonally you have written in that way [and] … you know its value absolutely" (pp. 148–149). To write well and truly is to be clear and faithful to the truth of the facts, of the news, of a situation, or of life itself. The pathways to such truth and clarity are not easily followed. They, like other items writers must reflect on and incorporate into their self-understanding, call for a moral dedication to technical proficiency, liveliness, originality, precision, and eloquence.

An inspirational text promoting the development of these capacities is George Orwell's (1956) "Politics and the English Language," in which he connected bad writing to bad politics. His complaints, uttered in the postwar period, were directed at fellow writers, whom he accused of writing texts that were opaque because they were riddled with clichés, abstractions, contrived expressions, and lazy formulations. "Modern English," he said, "is full of bad habits which spread by imitation and which can be avoided if one is willing to take the necessary trouble. If one gets rid of these habits one can think more clearly, and to think clearly is a necessary first step towards political regeneration" (p. 355). So Orwell admonished writers to speak plainly and clearly in the name of justice and the quality of political and intellectual life. As he wrote, "the slovenliness of our language makes it easier to have foolish thoughts" (p. 355).

Journalists Analyze and Judge

I have focused so far on authorship and craft. I think of the journalists I have in mind as reporters, writers, and critics, not to distinguish amongst journalists who report, those who write, and those who analyze and judge, but to state in a single series the faculties each journalist expresses as he or she composes such items as news briefs, narratives, scripts, editorials, and columns. In other words, I am speaking not of three kinds of journalists, but the functions embedded in the role of journalist.

> *All journalists engage in the functions of fact gathering, storytelling, and analyzing and/or arguing.*

The reporter in the journalist investigates and uncovers facts and prepares the way for the creation of texts; the writer in the same journalist writes faithful documents and stories based on these facts; the critic in the journalist provides the meaning of the facts of the stories, judges their significance, and explains why and how things happen. Some journalists do more of the first and less of the third. Some do more interpreting and analyzing than reporting.

However, in my view, all journalists who produce texts—for simple and straightforward purposes as well as for deeply complex ones—engage in the functions of fact gathering, storytelling, and analyzing or arguing. Satisfactory production of these texts reflects in degrees a moral understanding of the relationship between journalists and their fellow citizens, and a correspondingly moral understanding of their forensic, linguistic, and intellectual responsibilities. The miracle of journalism on its best days is that those of us who read, see, or listen to it are left with a composite picture of the state of things in the here and now. For this miracle to happen requires not only the creative and moral efforts of individual journalists, but also organization. Enter the word *media*.

The term refers in part to technology and in part to systems, organization, hierarchy, and control. It has risen to prominence, or so it would seem, on the head of broadcasting, first of radio and then of television, and has superseded and incorporated the term *press*. It is at least a word that in its broadest application calls into view circuses as well as civic life and culture. The circuses include Jerry Springer and reality TV, the public marriage and dating competitions, and other cultural derangements that are part and parcel of television's package. The term media also suggests a system of enormous scale and influence. Television, unlike the press, is less a backdrop to our lives than a powerful and ubiquitous presence in our daily experience. It is a source of entertainment, as well as a source of news and public commentary.

Television does not define journalism and is not the source of its basic character. That character was firmly established in the print media, and is now substantially incorporated into television. Nevertheless, television's influence as a medium of entertainment, over and above the matter of its ubiquity, is part of modern journalism's media reputation. Despite many fine examples of television journalism, it is evident that it enlarges, rather than shrinks, journalism's tendency to entertain rather than engage. Television has positioned tabloid journalism in the mainstream.

The alarm bells on tabloidization rang loud and clear during and after the O. J. Simpson trial, and even more loudly when the affair between President Clinton and Monica Lewinsky was unmasked. In the former case, there was a genuine belief that the cameras and commentators had interfered with the administration of justice, as a trial was turned into a circus. In the latter case, as so often happens, it was a print journalist who provided the basic fodder for the story. But television journalists, with the collaboration of politicians and lawyers, provided the country with a magnifying glass and an accelerator once the story got real legs. The magnifying glass gave it exceptional prominence. The accelerator gave it prominence in an hourly news cycle—as opposed to the 24-hour news cycle that marks print journalism—leading Carey (1998) to argue that the "speed of interaction among the institutions [of democratic government including the press] has its own multiplier effect. One day they could spin out of control" (p. 6). So an accelerated news cycle and the disposition to instant commentary as entertainment mark the broadcast news media in troubling ways that can be seen as television's gift to journalism.

I might add that these worries are connected to a much older concern—namely, the evolving pattern of ownership in the mass media. The early discussion was marked by a lament for the demise of independent publishers as they were bought out by newspaper chains. The theme of that discussion was that, in such chains, there was an unhealthy distance between head offices and news rooms with local responsibilities. That discussion continues, but with a new twist. The current discussion focuses more prominently on the possibilities of control arising from multimedia ownership and an emerging pattern of corporate control, such that the news media are being absorbed into even larger corporations whose commercial and political interests conflict materially with the work of journalists (McKercher, 2002). These corporations include Disney, an entertainment specialist.

The picture of journalism
formulated within the concepts
of craft and media are in conflict.

So the picture of journalism formulated within the concepts of craft and media are in conflict. In one setting, journalism is conceived as a democratic art that is a source of the connective tissue of a society of morally equal and self-governing citizens. In the other, the democratic art fights for its life within a system that either diminishes its effectiveness in the democratic system or threatens to bend it to commercial and ideological ends. It might be said that the image of journalism in media promotes a purist's despair and the craft image, by concentrating on the ideals out of which the practice is born, promotes naive idealism. Perhaps that is because each is stated too categorically. Still, useful clarifications arise from considering them separately as we imagine our duties and consider remedies.

Remedies and improvements called for by a careful reading of journalism's elements and an assessment of the systems within which it is practiced are in the hands of different groups. Journalists should think more actively of themselves as authors who are the custodians of precious ideals and rid themselves of a tendency to view their work, as some of their employers do and media notions strengthen, as mainly bureaucratic. They should be more conscious and appreciative of the complexities and moral significance of their work and allow themselves, through study and reflection, to be invigorated and inspired by the work of their most accomplished colleagues. Such forms of reflection and self-consciousness may not revolutionize journalism, but through the meanings they generate, should strengthen their attachment to journalism's democratic mission and diminish a tendency to cynicism and doubt.

As for corporate owners who are short on the virtues of citizenship because they are too obsessed with bottom lines, circulation figures, and ratings, they might be bullied into reading and absorbing the best codes of ethics. Such codes have been constructed from an understanding of the best journalistic practices and have evolved not only to guide journalists in the performance of their duties, but to strengthen the ability of journalists and editors to manage relations with business offices and departments of advertising within media companies. Journalism has always been circumscribed by interests which sometimes have reasons for wanting to rein journalists in. The difference now is that the constraining systems are larger and more powerful, and the outcomes potentially more threatening. So the audience for such codes should certainly include owners, new on the scene, who may promote a vision of journalistic work, regardless of medium, that is the source of journalism's and democracy's difficulties.

Public policy specialists and politicians should pay careful attention to the question of ownership and promote a reformulation, if that is what is necessary, of the rules governing monopolies and cartels. A greater measure of independence from government and industry is clearly desirable; a distancing from the entertainment business is equally desirable.

Finally, public-spirited citizens, network managers, owners, and, above all, journalists should work to ensure the security and impact of serious journalism by working to ensure that it is not marginalized. To conclude, I would say that all of this should be done with determination and patience. The structures of control and organization should not conflict with journalism's democratic mission. They should facilitate it. It is a matter of putting first things first.

References

Adam, S. (1993). *Notes towards a definition of journalism*. St. Petersburg, FL: Poynter Institute.

Carey, J. (1998, March/April). Publisher's note: The decline of democratic institutions. *Columbia Journalism Review*, p. 6.

Frye, N. (1964). *The educated imagination*. Bloomington: Indiana University Press.

Gardner, J. (1978). *On moral fiction*. New York: Basic.

Halberstam, D. (1965, January). Getting the story in Vietnam. *Commentary, 39*, 30–34.

Hemingway, E. (1935). *Green hills of Africa*. New York: Scribner's.

Hersey, J. (1986). The Legend on the license. *The Yale Review, 72*(2), 289–314.

Lyons, G. (1994, October). Fools for scandal: How the Times got Whitewater wrong. *Harper's*, pp. 55–63.

Kovach, B., & Rosenstiel, T. (2001). *The elements of journalism*. New York: Three Rivers.

Kymlicka, W. (2002). *Contemporary political philosophy, an introduction* (2nd ed.). Oxford, England: Oxford University Press.

McKercher, C. (2002). *Newsworkers unite, labor, convergence, and North American newspapers*. Lanham, MD: Rowman & Littlefield.

Orwell, G. (1956). Politics and the English language. In G. Orwell, *The Orwell Reader* (pp. 355–366). New York: Brace & World.

Ross, L. (2002). *Reporting back: Notes on journalism*. Washington, DC: Counterpoint.

Stone, R. (1988, June). The reason for stories. *Harper's*, pp. 71–76.

Journalistic Virtue and the Responsibilities
of Institutions
Stephanie Craft

Perhaps no event illuminates the tension between corporate and journalistic values better than the resignation of *San Jose Mercury News* publisher Jay Harris in 2001. Faced with ever-increasing pressure to boost profits, Harris quit rather than sacrifice quality to the budget cuts owner Knight-Ridder was demanding. Harris' resignation sparked a debate within journalism about the demands of the market, the needs of the public, and how to best reconcile them.

The climate is hardly welcoming to such reconciliation, however. As research on the newspaper industry by Cranberg, Bezanson, and Soloski (2001) demonstrated, increasingly "the business of news is business, not news" (p. 2). Indeed, any number of scholars has weighed in on the pernicious influence of the stock market, its demand for growth even in the short term, and allied problems created by media consolidation and ownership concentration on the practice of journalism. In simple terms, the purposes of journalism and business are seen to be at odds, and, to the extent the journalism side sees more reason to lament the situation, it is left to wonder just how to fix the system to avoid more damage. The assumption appears to be that only the journalism side bears responsibility for repair, and that the business side operates under its own rules, existing outside this sphere of responsibility. Too often, I argue, this lopsided approach results in solutions aimed at the wrong targets. No doubt, the behavior of individual journalists, in both moral and practical terms, could stand improvement. But that is true for everyone. Without attention to how the behavior of the corporations that create such a troublesome environment for journalism could be improved, solutions are unlikely at best.

A broadcast journalist who was part of a study examining the relationship between professional excellence and ethics summed up the difficult position of individuals in the current environment:

> Ethics has now been caught up in something so much bigger than any of us dreamed we would have to face, and that is the interest of the vast conglomerate that we now end up working for. (Gardner, Czikszentmihalyi, & Damon, 2001, p. 131)

Conglomerates, or even smaller media companies, have not expressed much interest in addressing the tension between journalism and business, however. Asked recently by a group of concerned journalists to eliminate stock options for news executives as a way of reducing profit pressures on the newsroom, media CEOs essentially responded, "Are you guys crazy?" (Moses, 2003, p. 22).

*Journalism occupies a privileged
position relative to profit only it its
corporate masters permit it*

Were this a clash of values between parties of roughly equal power, one
might argue it is temporary, that it is only a matter of time before the pen-
dulum swings from a greater concern for shareholder value to a greater
emphasis on journalism quality. But power is not equally distributed in the
case of news organizations and the corporations that own them. Journalism occupies a privileged position relative to profit only if its corporate
masters permit it.

In this essay, I hope to begin a discussion of moral agency as it applies to
the corporations that own the news media. The business ethics literature,
containing extensive examination of corporate moral agency, provides a
starting point. Subsequently, I will address unique features of the news industry that bear on this discussion. Along the way, I hope also to discuss
some of the superficial notions of virtue—particularly the "good journalism is good business" adage—that present obstacles to the search for
solutions.

The Business of Business Is Business?

To begin to address whether and how corporations are moral persons,
one must first overcome a conception of business as existing outside the
territory of moral concerns. Friedman's famous 1970 remark in the *New
York Times Magazine* that "the business of business is business" (see Solomon, 1992, p. 16) was enormously influential in shaping a notion of corporate social responsibility strictly limited to maximizing profit. To do
anything more in the name of responsibility, Friedman argued, was tanta-
mount to theft from a company's shareholders. One need look no farther
than current attempts to quantify journalistic quality and link it to profits
for evidence that "social responsibility equals profit maximization" thinking is prevalent in the media industry.

Even though Friedman's remark has considerable rhetorical power, the
conception of the nature of the corporation it suggests is not universally
shared. Solomon (1992), for example, defined the central problem in business ethics to be altering those conceptions of the nature of business and of
the corporation. His approach takes business to be a social practice, and
corporations to be communities of people working together for common
goals. Indeed, he argues, the general activities of business both depend
upon and presuppose the virtues and a basic sense of community.

Corporations, like individuals, are part and parcel of the communities that created them, and the responsibilities that they bear are not the products of argument or implicit contracts but intrinsic to their very existence as social entities. (Solomon, 1992, p. 149)

Just as individuals are products of community, so too are corporations inconceivable without community. Therefore, arguments such as those made by Friedman fail morally in that they attempt to isolate one set of responsibilities—duties to shareholders—from the larger community that gives such responsibilities meaning.

Solomon's approach echoed Alasdair MacIntyre's arguments for the application of virtue ethics to business. As Moore (2002) explained, MacIntyre defined practices as cooperative human activities that produce certain kinds of goods, particularly internal goods such as excellence (whichever kind of excellence is appropriate to the activity). Therefore, practices provide a place for the exercise of virtues. Institutions, on the other hand, are chiefly concerned with the achievement of external goods, such as power and profit. These goods are property, gained in a context of competition. Importantly, Moore's depiction of MacIntyre's schema showed practices as embedded in institutions, implying a dependence, and even vulnerability, of practices in relation to institutions. In most cases, MacIntyre argued, the distinction between practices and institutions will not be apparent; they form a single causal order. At other times, however, the kinds of goods each pursues come into conflict, often to the detriment of the practice. Put in a media context, the practice-institution distinction bears resemblance to Romano's distinction between fair media coverage of one story or another and a system of media coverage that is fair. In many cases, fairness can be said to exist at both levels. But there's also a sense in which such a single causal order cannot be depended upon. Certainly, the public often complains about what the media are doing without meaning to target the performance of individual journalists covering a particular story.

---

*It assigns moral importance
to corporations as the home
in which exercises of virtues
take place*

Moore (2002) applied MacIntyre's schema directly to business, asserting that business is a practice and corporations are the institutions in which business is embedded. Like any practice, then, business provides a place for the exercise of the virtues and for the achievement of excellence. The important implication of this description is that it assigns moral importance to corporations as the home in which exercises of virtues take place. That is, corporations take on some responsibility for the sustenance of practice, a responsibility that would appear to necessitate reining in desires for certain external goods if their pursuit damages practice. MacIntyre (1994) pointed out the potential for such imbalance. "Practices," he said, "are often distorted by their modes of institutionalization, when irrelevant considerations relating to money, power and status are allowed to invade the practice" (p. 289).

Examples of such distortion in the news media industry abound; an apparent denial both of the moral obligations of business generally and of corporate responsibilities to the individuals working within them.

What or Who Counts as a Moral Person?

If it is hard to imagine News Corp. or Enron as persons, think for a moment about how the activities of companies and collectives are described in everyday language: "Wall Street demands growth"; "Enron was greedy;" and so on. It is common, as Pruzan (2001) noted, to refer to an organization's goals and values, even while attributing the competencies necessary to form and act on such goals and values—reflection and evaluation, for example—only to individuals. Is this just a matter of misplaced metaphors? Pruzan argued not only that there are sound reasons to ascribe consciousness to organizations, but normative arguments for promoting a notion of organizational consciousness.

First, according to Pruzan (2001), organizations can be said to have the competency to develop values that are not just aggregations of the values of individuals in the organization. Here he also alluded to the role of community in identity-formation, much as Solomon (1992) and MacIntyre (1985) did. "Shared values are the criteria and standards that the organization and its stakeholders agree to use to reflect on the organization's identity, to evaluate whether the organization's actions are acceptable and to guide its development" (Pruzan, 2001, p. 276).

Second, given this self-reflective dialogue process, which is the basis for discovering values that can be said to express an organization's consciousness, management has a duty to act in a way that promotes those values. Only management has the legal power to make binding decisions, he noted, and only management "has the potential competency to make legitimate decisions by acting on behalf of the organization as a whole" (Pruzan, 2001, p. 280).

French (1984, 1991) asserted moral agency for the corporate entity itself and not just for the individuals who work in it. He also reminded us of the importance of taking corporations seriously in this regard, because of the power they hold: "Put simply, we live in a corporate world. Any responsibility theory that ignores corporations, or cannot reasonably account for what they do, is utterly inadequate" (French, 1991, p. 288).

In ascribing moral responsibility to corporations, French was asserting that corporations have the capacity for intentional action and that they can be held accountable for their actions. More specifically, the corporation can be a "noneliminatable subject in an ascription of moral responsibility" (French, 1984, p. 38), just as a man and not his arms, is the noneliminatable subject of blame if the man punches someone.

How can a corporation form an intention, and how can it act? French (1984) pointed to a Corporation's Internal Decision (CID) Structure as the locus of its ability to act intentionally. The CID Structure takes the form of organizational flow charts and stated policy; what French called the grammar and logic of corporate decision-making. These form the basis for determining whether an action was taken for corporate, versus individual, reasons:

> We can describe many events in terms of certain physical movements of human beings, and we also can sometimes describe those very events as done for reasons by those human beings, but further we can sometimes describe the same events as corporate and still further as done for corporate reasons that are qualitatively different from whatever personal reasons component members may have for doing what they do. (French, 1984, p. 47)

Therefore, if it makes sense, for example, to say that Knight-Ridder's CID Structure set the budget targets that Jay Harris refused to meet, then Knight-Ridder can be said to have intended to cut the budget and not just that the human beings working for Knight-Ridder intended to cut the budget. To be sure, those human beings may have intended to do other things, either in support of or in opposition to Knight-Ridder's plans. However, the existence of individual-level intention and responsibility does not preclude the possibility of corporate intention and responsibility, according to French's (1984, 1991) argument.

A collective may be more appropriately called to account for its behavior than the individuals who enact that behavior.

Perhaps most important for the purposes of this article, corporate moral agency comports with the experience of individuals working in media corporations and even of the public who consume the "products" of those corporations. That is, there seems to be a common sense or general feeling that a collective may be more appropriately called to account—or even ought to be held accountable—for its behavior than the individuals who enact that behavior. In the remaining pages, I will address how the notion of corporate moral agency might play out in the media industry, and suggest one reason it is particularly well suited to such an application.

Corporate Moral Agency and Competing Notions of the Media "Product"

What would it mean to call a media corporation a moral agent? The preceding discussion suggests that it means we can appropriately make moral judgments about its actions. To do so, we must accept that the corporation's organizational structures and policies form the basis for establishing its intent to act. Moreover, we must accept that its intended actions are not reducible to the actions of individuals, such as board members or managers.

I would argue that it is no more difficult to accept moral agency for media corporations than for any other kind of corporation. In fact, I might go so far as to suggest that it is easier. What I have in mind is that the corporations that own the news media straddle two realms, business and public service, in ways that other corporations do not, and in ways that both complicate and perhaps necessitate assigning moral agency to collectives. The complication is in the product the media makes and sells.

To offer a simple example, one might consider a corporation that makes detergent. Perhaps it is a large, vertically integrated corporation with employees, suppliers, factories, and customers all over the world. Although there is the potential for disagreement among the constituencies about how the corporation ought to make and sell its detergent, it is unlikely that the constituencies will disagree that it is, in fact, detergent that the corporation makes and sells. The same cannot be said for corporations that own news outlets. Cranberg et al. (2001) described how the market pressures that accompanied public ownership of newspapers helped to dramatically change notions about just what newspapers do:

> This was not like General Motors, with external market forces requiring GM to make better cars more efficiently in order to increase revenues and profits. It was instead as if the markets told GM to forget about the kind of cars it makes, and instead use them only as instruments for accomplishing other ends. Newspapers were encouraged, in other words, to see news simply as the engine for, or instrument of, delivering eyeballs for advertising, because the advertisers paid most of the bill anyway. (pp. 109–110)

Attempts to reconcile what McManus (1992) called the "conflict between corporate interest in selling and journalism's interest in serving the
public" (p. 198) have centered on demonstrating how journalism's interest
serves the corporate interest. I consider these attempts well intentioned
but, on some level, misguided. As I have argued elsewhere,

> the trouble comes not in considering whether good journalism sells or what
> kinds of resources should be devoted to creating good journalism if such
> journalism does not improve the bottom line. Rather, the trouble is that jour-
> nalism is not really conceived of as journalism at all, but as just another prod-
> uct alongside all the other products from which a diversified conglomerate
> expects to profit. (Davis & Craft, 2000, p. 223)

It is unclear, as Cohen (1999) pointed out, why the only seemingly legitimate reasons to be moral in business are those that link morality with self
interest, when it is generally accepted that individuals are not automatically relieved of acting morally when doing so is not in their self interest.
To link good ethics and good business is to imply that ethical behavior has
only instrumental value, Cohen argued.

In any event, a situation has developed in which news media corporations and the journalists who work for them do not share a notion of
what the corporation's product is or ought to be. Moreover, following
MacIntyre (1985), the lack of a shared idea about the purpose of the corporation, its product, frustrates the practice of journalism and of the corporation's ability to sustain that practice. The moral responsibility for
that harm rests with the institution, and the responsibility for bringing
the harm to light falls to the practice. Finding a corporation that accepts
such responsibility is difficult. For example, the chairman, CEO, and
president of Belo Corp, which has a number of print, broadcast, cable,
and Internet properties, tries to shift responsibility to a different collective—Wall Street: "We're not going to convince Wall Street that they
should treat our industry different," says Robert W. Decherd. "I don't
think we should spend a lot of time worrying about it and how we
should change it" (Moses, 2001, p. 21).

---

*It is not enough to say that the
way things are is not the way that
they ought to be.*

Comments like that can be disheartening to those who wish to revive
the public service purpose of journalism. Of course, it is not enough to

say that the way things are is not the way that they ought to be. What is needed is a way of reversing the formula in which journalism's interest is valuable only to the extent it can serve the corporate interest in profit. Corporate moral agency may represent one element in that new equation. Renewed attention to virtue and how it is exercised in the corporate context may be another. At a minimum, attention to the moral quality of decisions that affect the practice of journalism housed in the institution of the news media corporation might lay the groundwork for discussion.

I would argue that it is no more difficult, and arguably even easier, to accept moral agency for media corporations than for other kinds of entities. What I have in mind is that corporations that own news media straddle two realms, business and public service, in ways that other corporations do not. Although the framers of the U.S. Constitution could not have anticipated the modern media conglomerate, the press clause of the First Amendment suggests they thought of the press as an entity whose purpose was not solely or even predominantly profit generation, but public service. This implied responsibility both complicates and perhaps necessitates assigning moral agency to media corporations. The complication is in the product the media makes and sells.

References

Cohen, S. (1999). "Good ethics is good business" revisited. *Business and Professional Ethics Journal, 18*(2), 57–68.

Cranberg, G., Bezanson, R., & Soloski, J. (1984). *Taking stock: Journalism and the publicly traded newspaper company.* Ames: Iowa State University Press.

Davis, C., & Craft, S. (2000). New media synergy: Emergence of institutional conflicts of interest. *Journal of Mass Media Ethics, 15,* 219–231.

French, P. (1984). *Collective and corporate responsibility.* New York: Columbia University Press.

French, P. (1991). Corporate responsibility. In P. A. French (Ed.), *The spectrum of responsibility* (pp. 287–324). New York: St. Martin's.

Gardner, H., Csikszentmihalyi, M., & Damon, W. (2001). *Good work: When excellence and ethics meet.* New York: Basic.

MacIntyre, A. (1985). *After virtue.* London: Duckworth.

McManus, J. (1992). Serving the public and serving the market: A conflict of interest? *Journal of Mass Media Ethics, 7,* 196–208.

Moore, G. (2002). On the implications of the practice-institution distinction: MacIntyre and the application of modern virtue ethics to business. *Business Ethics Quarterly, 12*(1), 19–32.

Moses, L. (2003, February 3). Profiting from experience. *Editor and Publisher,* pp. 10–12; 21–22.

Phillips, M. (1992). Corporate moral personhood and three conceptions of the corporation. *Business Ethics Quarterly*, 2(4), 435–459.

Pruzan, P. (2001). The question of organizational consciousness: Can organizations have values, virtues and visions? *Journal of Business Ethics*, 29, 271–284.

Romano, C. (1998). All is not fair in journalism: Fairness to people vs. fairness to the truth. *Media Studies Journal*, 12(2), 90–95.

Solomon, R. (1992). *Ethics and excellence*. New York: Oxford University Press.

What Would Cronkite Do?
Journalistic Virtue, Corporate News,
and the Demise of the Fourth Estate
Elliot D. Cohen

The current climate of American journalism is fraught with incestuous relations between government and Fortune 500 corporations. The end product is an environment in which the watchdog of American democracy, the press, has become a docile representative of governmental authority. It is in this context that the concept of journalistic virtue should be defined, for it is in this context that the *raison d'etre* of the press has been called into question.

Although it is not news that the press, especially the broadcast media, have been largely influenced by its sponsors, the form of censorship and control examined in this article is that in which corporations in question own the media and are in business with government.[1] The problem lies in the incompatibility of corporate logic with the American media mission of holding the government accountable.

As John Ladd (1970) argued, the expectation that corporations act as morally responsible agents is a category mistake, one that now threatens the survival of a free press. Inasmuch as the central goal of a corporation is to maximize its bottom line (profit), whatever is most cost-effective in achieving this goal is predictably the path a corporation will follow. Legal regulations that constrain profit are therefore obstacles to be eliminated if this can be done cost-effectively. The quid pro quo of deregulation of media by government, procurement of defense contracts, and other financial arrangements in exchange for the media's adjusting the news to suit the purposes of government is thus a foreseeable corollary of the logic of corporate media decision-making.

How Government Uses Corporate Logic
to Control News Media

The American news media today are owned and operated by a relatively few major corporations (Miller, 2002). Of the primary news networks, MSNBC is under the dual corporate ownership of General Electric and Microsoft; CBS, formerly owned by Westinghouse, is now owned by Viacom; News Corporation owns Fox News; Disney Corporation now owns ABC; and AOL Time Warner owns CNN News.

In 2000, Microsoft created its Government division, which has as its main purpose the procurement of government contracts, especially lucrative ones such as those afforded by the U. S. Department of Defense. It has a history of government defense contract partnerships with such major defense contractors as General Dynamics (Kearney, 2000).

The same can be said of corporate giants like General Electric. For instance, according to investigative reporters, David Podvin and Carolyn Kay (2001), in June, 1999, shortly after George W. Bush declared his candidacy for the presidency, GE CEO Jack Welch was contacted by Bush's political advisor, Karl Rove, who guaranteed media deregulation in a manner that would mean large profits for GE and other media giants if Bush was elected. Welch reciprocated by making it well known throughout NBC News that the standard for promotion of journalists would be "outstanding contribution to the financial well being of General Electric," which included favorable coverage of George W. Bush. According to Podvin and Kay,[2] under these new administrative pressures, journalists like Tim Russert and Chris Matthews became model GE employees.

Other potential conflicts of interest include the supportive relationship presently enjoyed by corporate giants like Viacom-CBS, General Electric-NBC, and News Corporation-Fox with Bush appointee Michael Powell, Chairman of the Federal Communications Commission (FCC) and son of Secretary of State Colin Powell. The recent FCC ruling, which relaxed current ownership rules that regulate how much of the media market one company can own, underscores such potential for conflict of interest (Center for Digital Democracy, 2003).

Congress' extension of copyright length, underwritten and defended by the Bush administration and recently upheld by the U.S. Supreme Court (Greenhouse, 2003) may be still another instance of the quid pro quo between government and the corporate media. This change in copyright law has saved companies like Disney and AOL Time Warner hundreds of millions of dollars in movie royalties. Again, corporate logic dictates the lengths such corporations may be inclined to go to secure such legal victories.

Media codes of ethics typically instruct journalists to avoid conflict of interest, real or perceived (Elliott, 1997). Yet, if the companies by whom individual journalists are employed ignore such fundamental ethics, an obvious strain is placed upon individual journalists to practice within the strictures of professional ethics. It is this challenge that is likely to separate virtuous journalists from those who become conduits to unethical corporate media practices that undermine the essential purpose or end of a democratic press.

Virtuous Journalism and the End of a Democratic Press

When the First Amendment of the United States Constitution states that Congress shall make no law abridging freedom of speech, or of the press, it aims at protecting the press from governmental control. It is no accident that such a separation was placed foremost in the minds of the Founding Fathers, for it is a fundamental condition of a democratic nation. Democracy implies autonomous rule by the people. People cannot decide autonomously if they are not adequately informed. They cannot decide freely if government controls the flow of information they receive.

> *That the end [goal] of a democratic press is dissemination of information necessary for self-government is a tautology.*

Thus, a central purpose of news organizations in a democratic state, as distinct from a dictatorship, is to provide an independent source of information by which the governed can exert autonomous control over their own lives. That the end of a democratic press is dissemination of information necessary for self-government is a tautology. It is like saying that the purpose of a watchdog is to guard against trespass (a popular metaphor used to characterize the function of the press). This is just what it means to have a democratic press.

Within a democracy, the virtues of journalists include character traits that are conducive to the stated end of journalistic practice; just as the virtues of lawyers in an adversary system in a democracy are defined according to the promotion of substantive and procedural justice; or in medicine, according to the promotion of patient health. Following Aristotle (1941), these character traits can be defined as habits or dispositions to act in manners that advance the end of a democratic press. These habits involve dedication to principles of conduct that follow from the journalistic end of serving democracy. Insofar as this end is a moral end, these virtues and their corresponding principles are also moral. Even a cursory look at the variety of journalistic codes of ethics can give insight into what some of these virtues are. Thus, according to Article 1 of the *Statement of Principles* of the American Society of Newspaper Editors (1975), entitled Responsibility,

> The primary purpose of gathering and distributing news and opinion is to serve the general welfare by informing the people and enabling them to make judgments on the issues of the time. The newspapermen and women who abuse the power of their professional role for selfish motives or unwor-

thy purposes are faithless to that public trust. The American press was made free not just to inform or just to serve as a forum for debate but also to bring an independent scrutiny to bear on the forces of power in the society, including the conduct of official power at all levels of government.

According to the *Code of Ethics* of the Society of Professional Journalists (1996), under "Seek Truth and Report It," "Journalists should be honest, fair and courageous in gathering, reporting, and interpreting information." And they "should be free of obligation to any interest other than the public's right to know."

According to the Code of Ethics of the Radio-Television News Directors Association (2000), radio and television journalists should not "accept gifts, favors, or compensation from those who might seek to influence coverage"; and they should "present the news fairly and impartially, placing primary value on significance and relevance."

Journalists should cultivate habits of being responsible, loyal, fair, impartial, honest, and courageous in reporting the news. These virtues are also part of what it means to be a competent journalist. Journalistic competence cannot easily be severed from the moral routes of its ultimate mission. As Beauchamp and Klaidman (1992) suggested,

> Tape can be edited accurately, fairly, and objectively, or it can fail to meet these criteria. The editing cannot justifiably be called competent unless they are satisfied, which suggests that moral criteria are embedded in our very conception of competent journalistic practice. (p. 45)

Unfortunately, in the present environment, in which the news is being influenced by deals struck between government and corporate media, competence has been severely severed from its moral roots, and journalistic virtue has become an empty aspiration to which journalists have been paying lip service. Under the direction of its corporate and government masters, the press's silent acquiescence in the facade that it still honors its democratic charter may be among its greatest breaches of public trust. As Norman Solomon (2003) remarked, "deceptive propaganda can only succeed to the extent that journalists are gullible—or believe that they must pretend to be—while encouraging the public to go along with the charade" (p. 248). Putting on the facade of conducting business as usual, while delivering half the news or disseminating government propaganda, like fiddling while Rome burns, is neither honest, courageous, responsible, nor fair. Nor, in the end, is it likely to conduce to the public interest.

Aristotle (1941) held that the courageous or brave person acts according to the merits of the case and in whatever way the standards of right conduct direct, even if this involves great personal sacrifice. The professional standards of ethical conduct of journalists clearly direct journalists to avoid conflicts of interest and to remain steadfast to their primary democratic end. Under the present circumstances, this involves speaking out loudly against those powers surreptitiously working to undermine the public trust. This is what being a journalist in a democratic society means. This is non-negotiable and comes with the territory. It is not only cowardly to remain silent; it is journalistically incompetent.

Existentialist philosopher Jean-Paul Sartre (2000) stated that, "to choose to be this or that, is to affirm at the same time the value of what we choose" (p. 446). When a journalist chooses to work for a newspaper or a news corporation that is violating the public trust, he or she cannot avoid responsibility for whatever evils are worked by that network. In choosing the network, he or she is responsible for the violation and all that it entails. "I only work here" is not an adequate defense, because the journalist can choose not to work here. For Sartre, the journalist who acquiesces in news deception without admission of his complicity is a coward.[3]

When CBS news anchor, Dan Rather, appeared on the David Letterman show 6 days after the September 11 attack, he stated, "George Bush is the president, he makes the decisions," and "Wherever he wants me to line up, just tell me where. And he'll make the call." Eight months after the 9–11 tragedy, in a BBC television interview, Dan Rather of CBS admitted that he and other journalists had been intimidated out of "asking the toughest of the tough questions" for fear of being branded unpatriotic (Solomon, 2003, pp. 241–242).

On CNN's Reliable Sources, in an interview about whether the media have provided just coverage of protests against war in Iraq, Dan Rather guardedly stated,

> We've tried on the CBS Evening News, for which I'm responsible … to give the coverage we think is merited, but I'm open to the criticism. The White House and the administration power is able to control the images to a very large degree. It has been growing over the years. And that's the context in which we talk about, well, how much coverage does the anti-war movement merit? And I think it's a valid criticism it's been underreported. (CNN, March 9, 2003)

It is unfortunate that Rather's admissions were not voiced consistently and unequivocally before the American public. His willingness to continue as an anchor for CBS, despite these admissions, speaks more to his willingness to "line up" wherever he is told. To this extent, Rather betrayed the public trust that he, as a journalist, was supposed to uphold. Courage here would have meant standing on principles—those of honesty, responsibility, fairness, and loyalty to the journalistic faith—instead of allowing himself to be intimidated, even if this meant personal sacrifice.

In contrast is a journalist like National Public Radio's Daniel Schorr, who, in 1976, was fired by CBS News for sending a secret congressional intelligence report to the *Village Voice* when CBS refused to cover the story. According to Schorr, the network had struck a deal with the White House to go easy on the administration (Podvin & Kay, 2001).

Schorr placed the democratic mission of the press on a higher plane than his career. In the words of the Society of Professional Journalists (1996), a journalist should be "vigilant and courageous about holding those with power accountable." This appears to be what Schorr attempted to accomplish, and he was fired for the undertaking.

Arthur Kent, who earned the name "Scud Stud" for his coverage of the Gulf War, effectively ended his career with NBC when he publicly derided "Dateline" for its manipulation and re-editing of stories (Podvin & Kay, 2001). On January 30, 2003, and again on January 31, 2003, Paul Begala, the Democratic proponent of CNN's Crossfire, boldly denounced the news media for their politically biased and shoddy coverage of news surrounding the Bush administration (CNN, 2003).[4] His fate with the network is yet to be written.

In 2000, Walter Cronkite, world renowned for his forthrightness and unwavering commitment to a democratic press, helped to launch mediachannel.org, an Internet site devoted to the exploration of media concerns. He stated:

> As you know, I've been increasingly and publicly critical of the direction that journalism has taken of late, and of the impact on democratic discourse and principles. Like you, I'm deeply concerned about the merger mania that has swept our industry, diluting standards, dumbing down the news, and making the bottom line sometimes seem like the only line. It isn't and it shouldn't be.
>
> ...Pressure to go along, to get along, or to place the needs of advertisers or companies above the public's need for reliable information distort a free press and threaten democracy itself....
>
> We're always ready to speak out when journalists are at risk. But today we must speak out because journalism *itself* is at risk. (Cronkite, 2000)

Journalists who have taken the journalistic high road of speaking out about political concerns, despite personal risk and sacrifice, are more appropriate models of journalistic excellence than those who have earned their fame by being good corporate employees.

Journalists who have taken the journalistic high road of speaking out about political concerns, despite personal risk and sacrifice, are more appropriate models of journalistic excellence than those who have earned their fame by being good corporate employees. If the watchdog of democracy is to have teeth, then those who carry the torch must proceed without fear of intimidation from those who would distract them from their primary mission. If the press is to be restored to its rightful democratic throne, then a clear media voice must stand for separation of government and press. Virtuous journalists who care more for this journalistic faith than they do about their own reputations must carry the torch.

Democratizing the Press: The Challenge to Virtuous Journalists

The road to a democratic press in the rough wilderness of corporate oligopoly is not likely to be short and straight. As the history of those who have stood upon principle reveals, there are likely to be roadblocks and resistance offered by corporate and government benefactors of current media conditions. Journalists who have become allies, accomplices and servants of these benefactors are likely to stand against journalists who resist. Complacency with the status quo is likely to be rewarded by the powerful, and courage and patriotism made to look like cowardice and sedition. In this relentlessly duplicitous environment where fair is foul and foul is fair, change may be gradual and fraught with peril. So what can be done?

Schools of journalism can help by teaching the prospective purveyors of democracy the importance of their role in a free society. Emphasis on teaching the technical skills of editing, reporting, copyediting, and the like are empty without seeing these in their moral context. Ethics should not be an adjunct to instruction, as this artificially bifurcates morality from competence. Instead, the moral quality of technical competence should be flaunted and the skills viewed as empty corpses until the democratic spirit of the press breathes life into them.

Journalistic associations should be vigilantly vocal about the current state of American journalism. For example, the Society of Professional Journalists (1996) recognized "a special obligation to ensure that the public's business is conducted in the open and that government records are open to inspection." In this regard, it publishes a list of Red Flags on its web site that indicate when such freedom of information is in danger of being violated; for example, "Government files, which had been available, suddenly become unavailable" (Society of Professional Journalists, 2003). However, it should also be emphasized that the very news institutions entrusted with delivering the news may themselves be active participants in concealing the news from the public. This requires the generation of a new set of red flags that should send signals to individual journalists that the usurpation of freedom of information may, like an insidious Trojan Horse, be coming from within the news organization.

One effective safeguard against the demise of the democratic media is likely to be the emergence of nonprofit, noncommercial news organizations whose executive boards are free from conflict of interest and affiliation with government agencies, special interest groups, and powerful corporations, and which are not dependent upon corporate advertising funds for their survival (McChesney, 1998). Although many such organizations would likely require substantial government ("public") funding, the clear absence of the self-interested, bottom line logic that presently drives corporate media and undermines public trust, would greatly diminish opportunity for quid pro quo between government and media.[5]

In the 17th century, Thomas Hobbes (2003) wrote,

> It is annexed to the sovereignty [government] to judge of what opinions and doctrines are averse, and what conducing to peace; and consequently, on what occasions, how far, and what men are to be trusted withal in speaking to multitudes of people; and who shall examine the doctrines of all books before they be published. For the actions of men proceed from their opinions, and in the well governing of opinions consists of the well governing of men's actions in order to their peace and concord. And though in matter of doctrine nothing ought to be regarded but the truth, yet this is not repugnant to regulating of the same by peace. (pp. 209–210)

It is instructive to note that, in this passage, Hobbes was discussing the way a successful dictator should deal with the media. His argument that truth should be "regulated" for the sake of "peace" is an old dictatorial saw, more commonly these days coached in terms of "national security." This is not the language of democracy or of a free society. Dictatorships have always sought to silence or control the press, and it is one of the first things they do when they come to power. A red flag that we may have budding dictatorship is that we have a press too intimidated to speak out. Recalling the confessional of Dan Rather, there is much need now for virtuous journalists to come forth and speak out. This is not optional. It is urgent and of the essence of what it means to be a journalist in a democracy.

Notes

1. "Business" includes the quid pro quo of agreements for mutual advantage without any formal contract or monetary transaction. This form of mutuality between government and media is not new. For example, during Richard Nixon's 1972 reelection campaign, major newspapers promised Nixon edito-

rial support in exchange for his support of the Newspaper Preservation Act. As a result, newspaper corporations were able to attain monopolies in many American cities (see McChesney, 2000). As I suggest in the following, such quid pro quo between corporate media and government appears to be widespread in the broadcast media.

2. Podvin and Kay are investigative reporters for MakeThemAccountable.com, an on line news source aimed at accountability in media and government.

3. "Those who hide their complete freedom from themselves out of a spirit of seriousness or by means of deterministic excuses, I shall call cowards" (Sartre, 2000, p. 448).

4. In particular, on January 31, he said the following:
   Last night I reported to you on the breath-taking hypocrisy of President Bush, praising the work of the Boys and Girls Clubs, calling them "little beacons of light," then cutting off their electricity by reducing their budget $10 million. I suggested that none of the major media would have the guts to report President Bush's brazen bad faith. I was wrong a little. One reporter, Mike Allen, at one newspaper, *The Washington Post*, wrote one sentence about it. Nothing in *The New York Times*, nothing on the AP, nothing on CNN, except here on Crossfire, or any of the other so-called news networks. The lesson: You can bask in the glow of a wonderful group even if you've cut its budget, because the press corps is so cowed by the Bush White House, you can almost hear them moo. President Bush, of course, could not be reached for comment. He was too busy laughing his ass off.

5. Although nonprofit media exist today, such media are largely dependent upon corporate advertisers and receive insufficient public funding. This is in comparison to other nations such as England and Japan, which maintain a more robust and autonomous nonprofit media (McChesney, 1998).

References

American Society of Newspaper Editors. (1975). *ASNE statement of principles*. Retrieved July 1, 2003, from http://www.asne.org/kiosk/archive/principl.htm

Aristotle. (1941). Nichomachean ethics (W. D. Ross, Trans.). In R. McKeon (Ed.), *Basic works of Aristotle* (pp. 927–1112). New York: Random House.

Beauchamp, T. L., & Klaidman, S. (1992). *The virtuous journalist*. New York: Oxford University Press.

Center for Digital Democracy. (2003, June 2). FCC deals a blow to diversity and democracy. Retrieved July 1, 2003, from http://www.democraticmedia.org/news/june2.html

CNN. (2003, January, 31). Jerry Springer, Ann Coulter, debate war with Iraq, domestic policy. *Crossfire*. Retrieved July 1, 2003, from http://www.cnn.com/TRANSCRIPTS/0301/31/cf.00.html

CNN. (2003, March 9). Were Whitehouse reporters used as cogs in pro-war machine? What is life like for journalists on front lines? *Reliable sources*. Retrieved July 1, 2003, from http://www.cnn.com/TRANSCRIPTS/0303/09/rs.00.html

Cronkite, W. (2000, February 3). Walter Cronkite on the media; And the Media Channel. *MediaChannel.org*. Retrieved July 1, 2003, from http://www.mediachannel.org/originals/cronkite.shtml

Elliott, D. (1997). Conflicts of interest. In E. D. Cohen & D. Elliott (Eds.), *Journalism ethics* (pp. 91–96). Santa Barbara, CA: ABC-CLIO.

Greenhouse, L. (2003, January 16). 20-year extension of existing copyrights is upheld. *New York Times*. Retrieved July 1, 2003, from http://www.nytimes.com/2003/01/16/business/media/16BIZC.html?todaysheadlines

Hobbes, T. (2000). Dictatorship. In E. Cohen (Ed.), *Philosophers at work: Issues and practice of philosophy* (2nd ed., pp. 205–210). Fort Worth, TX: Harcourt.

Kearney, P. (2000, September 27). Microsoft does business with the Department of Defense. *TheStranger.com*. Retrieved July 1, 2003, from http://www.thestranger.com/2000-09-21/city5.html

Klaidman, S., & Beauchamp,T. (1992). The virtuous journalist: Morality in journalism. In E. D. Cohen (Ed.), *Philosophical issues in journalism* (pp. 39–49). New York: Oxford University Press.

Ladd, J. (1970). Morality and the ideal of rationality in formal organizations. *Monist, 54*, 488–516.

McChesney, R. (1998). Making media democratic. *Boston Review, 23*, 4–10. Retrieved July 1, 2003, from http://www.uiowa.edu/~c036088/mcchesney.html

McChesney, R. (2000). *Rich media, poor democracy: Communication politics in dubious times.* New York: New Press.

Miller, M. C. (2002). The big ten media giants. In P. Phillips (Ed.), *Censored 2003: Media democracy in action* (pp. 231–240). New York: Seven Stories.

Podvin, D., & Kay, C. (2001, October). Democracy, General Electric style. *Midwest Today*. Retrieved July 1, 2003, from http://www.midtod.com/exclusives/jack-welch.phtml

Radio-Television News Directors Association. (2000). *RTNDA Code of Ethics.* Retrieved July 1, 2003, from http://www.rtndf.org/ethics/coe.shtml

Sartre, J.(2000). Existentialism. In E. D. Cohen (Ed.), *Philosophers at Work* (2nd ed., pp. 444–449). Fort Worth, TX: Harcourt.

Society of Professional Journalists. (1996). *SPJ code of ethics.* Retrieved July 1, 2003, from https://www.spj.org/ethics_code.asp

Society of Professional Journalists. (2003). Red flags to violation of freedom of information (FOI). Retrieved July 1, 2003, from http://www.spj.org/foia_opendoors_flags.asp

Solomon, N. (2003). Media war and the rigors of self-censorship. In P. Phillips (Ed.), *Censored 2003* (pp. 241–253). New York: Seven Stories.

Journal of Mass Media Ethics, *19*(3&4), 276–292
Copyright © 2004, Lawrence Erlbaum Associates, Inc.

Professional–Client Relationships: Rethinking Confidentiality, Harm, and Journalists' Public Health Duties

Renita Coleman
Louisiana State University

Thomas May
Medical College of Wisconsin

❏ *Journalists seldom consider the layers of those affected by their actions; third parties such as families, children, and even people unlucky enough to be in the wrong
place at the wrong time. This article argues for consideration of the broader group,
considering a range of options available for doing their duty to inform the public
while also minimizing harm to others. Journalists might compare themselves with
other professions that have similar roles, such as anthropologists, on such issues as
confidentiality and disclosure. A broader lesson is the value of applying different
views, theoretical frameworks, and starting points to the ethical issues in any
profession.*

The definition of a professional is one who is devoted to the service of
the public, above and beyond material incentives (Larson, 1977). Doctors,
lawyers, nurses, accountants, clergy, and social workers, among others, are
included in this category of professions. Journalists often think of themselves as professionals, even though they are not subject to specific educational requirements, licensing, and formal means of censure in the way
that other "true" professionals are. Nevertheless, the spirit of the term is
appropriate for journalists, not only because they serve the public interests, but also because of their relationships with others that embody additional rights, responsibilities, and expectations. In medicine and other
professions, these "others" are referred to as clients, and there is much discussion of professional–client relationships. Although journalists consider
the public—their audience—to be their primary "client," not an individ-

ual, the way the medical, legal, accounting, and other professionals do, journalists do have client-like relationships with others, including their sources and the subjects of their stories. Under this rubric, there is much discussion of the dilemmas that journalists face when trying to satisfy often competing interests, and to prevent harm to individuals and the public.

In this article, we explore the ethical ramifications of the professional–client relationship across three professions that are alike in some respects and very different in others. The common ground and places where the three part ways in terms of theoretical frameworks, obligations, and responsibilities are particularly relevant analogies for seeing each profession in a different light. Specifically, we first examine the conflict between a physician's duty to maintain confidentiality and a journalist's duty to disclose. Next, we compare journalists' view of client relationships to a profession with similarities to journalism—anthropology—that uses a very different starting point for dealing with others. Finally, we present an argument for a broader definition of journalism's clients to include "third parties" that are one layer further from sources and subjects of news stories.

The Intersection of Journalism and Medicine

In discussions of professional–client relationships, the issue of confidentiality frequently surfaces. Doctor–patient privilege regarding medical information is one of the most strongly protected laws in American society. The question of confidentiality in the doctor–patient relationship arises most dramatically when a celebrity or public personality experiences a health problem. Rumors circulate, and journalists often enter the picture when they are expected to investigate the legitimacy of these rumors. Such investigation often involves questioning physicians caring for a patient, placing the physician in the awkward position of either lying, violating the patient's confidentiality, or not commenting (which allows the rumors to continue). In addition, questions are raised about the journalist's own obligations to report "private" information about an individual's health condition. What information does the public have a right to know, and what information should be off limits? It is understood that celebrity comes with the sacrifice of privacy in many areas of life; however, as a society we are reluctant to regard health matters as one of the areas in which privacy must be sacrificed.

Confidentiality Versus the Greater Public Good

The most common argument for violating confidentiality when public personalities are concerned involves responsibility to the public. When the health condition of a celebrity or public figure is known, it is argued, it educates the public about this condition, resulting in benefits for others suffering from this malady. These benefits derive from two sources: First, greater public awareness of, and education about, the condition in question can help remove any stigma attached to that condition. The clearest example of this phenomenon can be seen in Magic Johnson's public disclosure that he tested positive for HIV. Prior to this disclosure, those who suffered from HIV were widely regarded as people to be avoided. Johnson's disclosure changed this, and even led to (reluctant) acceptance of HIV positive individuals participating in team sports (through his return to the NBA several years later). Johnson raised public awareness and understanding of his condition and prompted greater public acceptance of people with HIV through a better understanding of the limitations on how HIV might be spread.

Second, disclosure that a public personality suffers from a particular condition or affliction often results in greater resources devoted to the cure or treatment of that condition. Two prominent examples illustrate this: Michael J. Fox's disclosure that he suffers from Parkinson's disease, and Christopher Reeve's role in promoting research into treatment of spinal cord injuries. Each has testified before Congress concerning the need for greater biomedical research funding and promoted research as a social priority. We will ignore, for the purposes of this article, questions about the fairness of a condition suffered by a celebrity receiving greater resources and conditions that lack a celebrity spokesperson do not. Instead, we will focus only on the possible benefits of this, as it is this that argues for disclosure.[1]

Physicians' Obligations—A New Context for an Old Principle

The reasons we are, and should be, hesitant to require the sacrifice of privacy in health matters for a public personality are the very same reasons we wish to protect privacy in the doctor–patient relationship in general. These are as follows:

1. Dignity and respect for autonomy. Control over access to information about oneself is an integral part of developing intimacy. Those closest to us have access that others do not. Think of how this applies in our lives; sharing feelings, wishes, and plans that are not commonly known is at the heart of our most intimate relationships. This may be even more important for a celebrity, for whom so many realms of life are open to public scrutiny.

2. A need for accuracy. Without strong confidentiality, accurate accounts of personal history, symptoms, and risk factors may be lacking. This

is acknowledged explicitly in the American Medical Association (AMA) Code of Ethics (2001):

> The information disclosed to a physician during the course of the relationship between physician and patient should remain confidential to the greatest possible degree. The patient should feel free to make a full disclosure of information to the physician so that the physician may most effectively provide needed services.

In short, the AMA code acknowledges that without full and accurate personal information, proper diagnosis, testing, and treatment may not occur; and that without strong confidentiality, full and accurate personal information may not be conveyed.

Although a strong obligation of confidentiality is an integral part of the doctor–patient relationship, there are limits.

Although a strong obligation of confidentiality is an integral part of the doctor–patient relationship, there are limits. The most famous limit to confidentiality is the Tarasoff (1976) case, which resulted in a national expansion of the duty-to-warn laws. In this landmark case, a psychiatrist learned of a client's intention to kill a young woman, but failed to warn her of the potential threat because laws regarding doctor–patient privilege prevented him from revealing what the client had said. Tragically, the young woman was murdered. The principle that results from the Tarasoff case acknowledges that confidentiality can, and sometimes should, be broken when significant harm is posed to a third party.

For the benefits just described to serve as a justification for the violation of confidentiality on the basis of public responsibilities, however, we must establish that a failure to benefit others in this way constitutes a harm analogous to those recognized by the Tarasoff (1976) principle as overriding the principle of confidentiality. The initial problems that arise in this regard concern the lack of specificity in who would be harmed by keeping the celebrity's health condition secret, and lack of intention to cause such harm. Most ethicists agree that this Tarasoff principle requires, in some form, (a) an identifiable individual to whom harm is posed, and (b) supporting action or ideation of overt action to harm a third party, though there is extensive disagreement about exactly what constitutes these, as well as the significance of the harm necessary to break confidentiality.

These problems, however, can be overcome. The Tarasoff (1976) requirements of a specific individual to whom harm is posed, as well as the supporting action or overt ideation, are requirements meant to establish the
credibility of the threat of harm. This is necessary because, where one seeks
to override basic rights, and the right of privacy in health matters is surely
a widely regarded basic moral and legal right, the burden or argument
must fall on the one who seeks to override these rights. Therefore, it falls on
whoever is to break confidentiality to establish the credibility of a threat of
harm, and thus the Tarasoff requirements. If the credibility of a threat
of harm can be established even without specificity and supporting action
or ideation, however, this credible threat of harm should play the same role
as Tarasoff threats.

One situation where expanded Tarasoff requirements might be used is
in the case of a U.S. President. At least 14 of 19 U.S. Presidents in the 20th
Century have suffered from significant illness while in the White House,
which either did, or had the potential to, affect their capacity to function
in the role of President. Public knowledge of the condition of each varied, but in almost every case, information was either withheld, or information that was made available to the public was packaged and significantly misleading. For example, following Woodrow Wilson's
debilitating stroke in October 1919, a stroke that completely paralyzed
the left side of his body, the White House physician issued the following
statement, "The President had a fairly good night ... but his condition is
not good this morning." A few days later, "... his condition is less favorable today, and he has remained in bed throughout the day ... it was determined that absolute rest is essential for some time." Nowhere was it
even suggested that he had suffered a stroke. Not even the Cabinet was
informed about the true nature of the President's condition. Many histo-
rians believe that Wilson's incapacity is to blame for the failure of the
League of Nations, which, it is argued, if successful might have averted
World War II.

We argue that a deeper consideration of the ethical ideas underlying the
Tarasoff (1976) principle shows that this is applicable to Presidential illness. In the case of incapacity of a U.S. President, there is a very credible
threat of harm, both to the U.S. population as well as the international community. An incapacitated President cannot act in ways that he or she otherwise might. Wilson's incapacity, for example, resulted in many matters being put on hold, laws not signed, and actions not taken: all in the context of
a country in the throes of postwar crisis, soaring inflation, high unemploy-
ment, and labor strife.

We now live in a nuclear world, and the President of the United States is
commander-in-chief of the most powerful military in the history of the
world. The types of mood changes and personality changes that resulted

from Wilson's and even Roosevelt's health problems could have significant, in some cases unspeakable, negative ramifications.

There is good reason, then for the application of Tarasoff-type (1976) limitations on the doctor–patient relationship between a President of the United States and the White House physician, and therefore, good reason for developing mechanisms for making the position of White House physician more accountable to the public. This is not to say that the relationship between President and White House physician should be transparent, open to full public disclosure; the Tarasoff principle itself recognizes the importance of confidentiality absent a significant, credible threat of harm.

The Distinction Between Positive and Negative Duties

The more fundamental problem concerns whether failure to benefit constitutes harm. The key to understanding this debate is the issue of how intrusive a positive duty to prevent harm would be (May, 2002). In the context of our discussion here, the intrusiveness in question concerns how intrusive a positive duty to promote the public health, a duty that might require public disclosure of personal health information if such disclosure could prevent harm to others suffering from similar maladies, would be for the individual who has this duty. Joel Feinberg (1984) discussed extensively the nature of positive and negative (in Feinberg's terminology, "affirmative" and "prohibitive") duties in terms of their intrusiveness on the aims of the individuals on whom these duties might fall. Feinberg argued that positive duties are not necessarily more intrusive than negative duties. As an example, Feinberg pointed to the fact that certain prohibitive requirements, like the prohibition of driving more than 10 miles per hour in a school zone, significantly limit one's options. On the other hand, an affirmative duty for a bystander to warn a blind person that he is about to step into an open manhole "requires only a spoken word, which hardly limits his other options at all" (p. 163). Feinberg stated:

> When one compares the degree of intrusiveness of a requirement to act … against that of a prohibitive restriction … one is as likely to find one or the other more restrictive of liberty, depending not on whether it is affirmative or prohibitive, but rather on its impact on one's options. (pp. 163–164)

Nonetheless, at a political and legal level, U.S. society does not view "positive duties" to prevent harm to be similar to "negative duties" not to cause harm. Heidi Malm, for example, believed that the difference between the stringency of the duty not to cause harm and the duty to prevent harm is due to the fact that our society places great value on autonomy, and "it simply would not be fair to require persons to risk sacrificing their most important aims or interests in order to prevent a potential harm which they had no responsibility for initiating" (cited in Feinberg, 1984, p. 168). This general perception seems to be the approach recognized by the political (especially legal) structures in the United States, which views positive requirements as more demanding on the aims of individuals, creating what Feinberg characterized as a perception that establishing a duty to aid is inconsistent with liberal social arrangements. This perception is so fundamental, in fact, that, as Feinberg stated:

> The common-law tradition has left unpunished even harmful omissions of an immoral kind—malicious failures to warn a blind man of an open manhole, to lift the head of a sleeping drunk out of a puddle of water, to throw a rope from a bridge to a drowning swimmer, to rescue or even report the discovery of a small child wandering lost in the wood, and so on. (Feinberg, 1984, p. 127)

It seems, then, that unless one can demonstrate a likelihood of direct harm to a third party (e.g., in Tarasoff, 1976, cases or in cases where an individual is known to have exposed a third party to an infectious disease), society does not view the failure to prevent harm through public disclosure of personal health information as sufficient to override individual autonomy rights to withhold such information. Given the strong social, political, and legal duties of confidentiality in medicine, the physician's obligation should be to maintain confidentiality.

This leaves open, however, the question of a journalist's obligations in reporting information about a celebrity's personal health condition, and the balancing of potential harms to both society, and to the celebrity in question.

Journalists' Obligations—Drawing From a Similar Profession

Two questions arise from recognizing that public disclosure of a celebrity's medical problems might have positive social effects: First, what are the obligations of the treating physician in regard to maintaining confidentiality; and second, what are the obligations of journalists in regard to reporting of confidential information?

Given the context of public disclosure of personal information to promote a greater societal good, it might be useful to consider the analogy of anthropological reporting of data to see how this might and might not apply to our own context. Journalists have three basic similarities to anthropologists. First, the professional seeks out the client rather than the client seeking out the professional. Second, both journalists and anthropologists employ noninductive methods. Both conduct interviews, observe, and write up their accounts for a larger audience to help understand some aspect of culture. And third, the work of both journalists and anthropologists does not yield generalizable knowledge. Both professions are more concerned with specific cases and instances, although larger claims can be read into that.

> *[Unlike anthropologists]*
> *journalists ... are never quite*
> *clear about who the client is.*

The dissimilarities between journalists and anthropologists include how they define their relationship to others; that is, who is the client? For anthropologists, the client is the informant—what they call the sources of their stories—not the larger reading public or the consumer of anthropological research. Journalists, on the other hand, are never quite clear about who the client is. Journalists' references to "the public" are often self-serving and vague. The client isn't promised confidentiality or informed consent the way anthropologists do for their clients. Anthropologists promise their informants confidentiality and take great care to explain the risks and benefits to them and gain their informed consent. Journalists, on the other hand, often have a relationship with sources based on deception. For them, the client is a rhetorical device used to justify certain kinds of conduct. It is far from informed consent.

One example involves a time that Stanford University Communication professor Ted Glasser was writing a story on ombudsmen. Glasser tells the story:

> I called an ombudsman I knew and told him I was working on a column and I was very vague about what the article was about. If I told him the truth, I knew he wouldn't be as candid as I wanted. The result was that after the article came out, he didn't speak to me for years.

This is an everyday occurrence for journalists, not the exception. A promise of confidentiality in journalism is claimed to be presumptively wrong and is only offered rarely. This is a very different starting point than that of anthropologists. Anthropologists assume far more responsibilities for the consequences of their work than journalists want to accept. This has to do with a more sophisticated appreciation for anthropologists' role in society than journalists' and their role in society. Journalists often claim their status requires them to disregard consequences because they are concerned with getting the information out.

Another claim about relationships with larger publics authorizes the anthropologist to move from the role of disseminator of information to the role of advocate. This is an option their code of ethics gives them. However, this is very different from journalists, who have only recently begun acknowledging and taking into account the political and social framework. Freedom of the press isolates and insulated journalists from society in such a way that accountability is lost.

Journalists have an obligation to reflect on their own interests. These kinds of discussions would serve journalists well in terms of clarifying their relationships with the public and their sources. The point is not to impose a social science system of informed consent on journalists, but to start a discussion about journalists' obligations and relationships, and to remind us that we have walked away from these discussions rather than take them up.

Obligations and Limitations of Journalists— Overlooked Third Parties

When journalists do take up discussions about their obligations and interests, most of the focus is on the public at large or the individual who is the source or subject of the news story. However, others once removed can also play a role in this relationship. In this section, we explore an expanded definition of third parties and their role in the journalism realm.

Third parties are most often defined as family members, friends, and others significant to the client. The third parties that journalists must deal with, including family members, may not be so different from the third parties that medical professionals, attorneys, and other professionals encounter. Where journalists are concerned, the definition of third parties can be widened to include clergy members, teachers, social workers, law enforcement, and justice officials. In some cases, even politicians and celebrities have entered the picture as third parties. When children are involved, an additional ethical consideration, that of protecting the weak, complicates the issue.

*We argue for a wider definition
of stakeholders to include
consideration of third parties
beyond the primary stakeholders
in journalists' ethical decisions.*

Often, third parties, or people just outside the inner circle of journalists and their sources or subjects, are not considered when journalists make decisions. Harm can come to third parties, just as it can to primary sources or subjects of a story, as a result of what journalists publish. Furthermore, failure to consider third parties can be problematic in other ways for news organizations. We argue for a wider definition of stakeholders to include consideration of third parties beyond the primary stakeholders in journalists' ethical decisions. A variety of cases offer examples of third parties in journalism dilemmas, and help us explore the rights and responsibilities of the media.

Causing Harm to Third Parties

The most recent and poignant example of the effects of media coverage on third parties came in a letter to the children of the Columbia space shuttle tragedy from the now-grown daughter of an astronaut killed in the 1986 Challenger explosion: "My father died a hundred times a day on televisions all across the country ... . It should have been a moment of private grief, but instead it turned into a very public torture," wrote the daughter of astronaut Dick Scobee. Of the media she said, "They can't know how painful it is to watch your Mom or Dad die several times each day. If they knew how much pain it caused, they would stop" (Fulghum, 2004). Susan Sontag (1977) was wrong, it appears; the shock of photographed atrocities does not wear off with repeated viewings when those viewing them are the loved ones of the people in the photos.

Of course, Sontag was referring to the mass audiences becoming emotionally numb to shocking photographs. It doesn't always take the years that she refers to for the public to reach an emotional saturation point. It is not hard to imagine the viewing audience becoming immune in a matter of hours after watching the endless repetition of a few seconds of video showing a plane crashing into the World Trade Center. However not, apparently, for the friends and relatives of those who died.

This discussion is not meant to imply that journalists should never air video or run a photo that would be painful to some; of course journalists must show the video or photo and even show it more than once. To not do so would be to abandon the press' primary responsibility to inform the public. The third parties affected by the image may even encourage its use so the world may know what happened. What this discussion targets is the use of visuals that have reached the point of being used more as a logo than as information—a slide graphic over the anchor's shoulder, for example. It is then that journalists should begin to ask questions about its continued use.

Bok's (1989) framework for ethical decision making offers a guide for asking those questions. It is based on two premises: empathy for the people involved and maintaining social trust. Journalists' primary responsibility of informing the public falls under the rubric of social trust. Even if the families of the dead astronauts are harmed by viewing the disaster over and over again, the public has a right and a need to know what happened, and that need and right outweigh the families' need for privacy. Questions of empathy for the people involved may be explored using Bok's three steps for ethical decision making. The first question, searching one's conscience, may be satisfied for journalists who feel they are fulfilling their primary duty to inform.

Bok's (1989) second and third steps are more problematic. For example, conducting a hypothetical public discussion with those involved will certainly raise the question of causing harm to third parties. Journalists should acknowledge there is little benefit in showing the video, once the public has been well informed by the story being told repeatedly and video shown again and again. Journalists know that audiences stop reacting emotionally when the images cease to be novel; neither do audiences gain new information from visuals they have seen a hundred times. Audiences may even say they are tired of seeing the plane fly into the tower for the umpteenth time, while third parties describe the pain it causes them. If journalists are honest, they will admit that showing the footage repeatedly or rerunning a frequently used photo mainly serves their medium's need for visuals. The story may still be unfolding with new information, but no new images. Or, the new images are not as gripping and attention getting as the original footage. The best, and easiest, visuals are the original ones. Journalists must weigh their desire for easy, spectacular images against the harm that may be done to third parties. In such a public discussion, journalists, who may not even be aware of an ethical dilemma, should ask themselves about the rightness of their actions with regard to others they are not used to considering.

Bok's (1989) other step, seeking expert advice for alternatives, explores the possibility of other ways to achieve the same goal that will not raise the ethical issue of harming third parties. Alternatives may not be as easy to obtain or as visually exciting, but that needs to be weighed against causing emotional harm to third parties.

When Third Parties Are Children

Most journalists do not mean to harm third parties with actions such as repeated use of visuals, but unintended harm is one of the most difficult to spot aspects of ethical dilemmas. When those third parties are children, the added duty of protecting weaker persons is imposed (Mill, 1859/1956; Rawls, 1971).

Much like the ethical dialogue of Bok (1989), Rawls recommended deliberations among the stakeholders behind a "Veil of Ignorance," where none of the stakeholders knows what status each will have after the decision is made. Under this framework, weaker parties, such as children, are usually protected. Evidence usually must be overwhelming that the welfare of the entire group would be bettered for reasonable people to make a decision at the expense of weaker parties. Thousands of years of ethical thinking, and even laws, have agreed that children deserve special protection.

Journalists consider children's welfare when those children are their sources (Smith-Fullerton, 2002), but when those small faces are once removed, the discussion about them frequently disappears. For example, when *USA Today* revealed that former tennis star Arthur Ashe had AIDS, Ashe's privacy wasn't the only thing being invaded; at the time, Ashe had a 5-year-old daughter (Day, 2000). Most of the postmortem discussions among journalists about the decision to publish revolved around privacy and public figures, voyeurism or news value, and public education. Some included discussion of harm to Ashe himself, but few considered the third parties, including his minor children.

A consideration of the children in this case may have made the difference in the decision. After all, it was arguable that by 1992, the mere knowledge of another celebrity with AIDS could do little to lessen the stigma or educate the public.

Requests to Withhold

Withholding publication of something, such as a story or repeated visual, usually involves third parties in a more obvious way. There are many examples of third parties, rather than the primary stakeholders, asking the press not to run a name, photograph, or some piece of information. Borden (1996) examined one such case where a family's rabbi asks a newspaper not to run a photograph of the sheet-draped body of a young man killed in a car accident. His rationale was that it would cause the family too much grief.

When these pleas come from third parties rather than the primary stakeholders in an ethical dilemma, do they carry more or less weight? The consideration of self-interest is somewhat removed by having a third party make the request. But when the third party is someone with influence, such as a doctor, lawyer, or clergy person, is the request more compelling?

Invisible Third Parties

Sometimes, third parties are difficult to recognize even when one is trying. Consider, for example, the case of a TV news magazine's hidden camera investigation of a rehabilitation hospital. The show deliberately blurred the faces of patients who had been abused so as to conceal their identity and protect their privacy (Lambeth, 2000). However, what of the employees, some of whom were clearly identified in the photos? Readers may well infer guilt by their mere association with allegations in the story. It is well documented that people misremember negative things about individuals when their photos are juxtaposed with stories about negative events (Grimes & Drechsel, 1996). The individuals whose faces were shown were never given a fair trial, so to speak.

Harm to Journalists

Although important, causing harm to others isn't the only issue journalists must consider in relation to third parties. Occasionally, third parties consider the actions by the media so egregious that they seek relief through the courts. In Puerto Rico, a police official sued the media for defamation and then his wife sued for emotional distress even though she was never mentioned in the article (Anonymous, 1994). In ruling not to dismiss the case, the court recognized that the damage defamation can do is not limited to the person who claims to have been defamed. This is a valuable lesson for journalists about extending the scope of who qualifies for consideration as a third party.

Another situation involving third parties that can result in harm to journalists sometimes arises when a third party obtains information illegally, or the information is protected by legal privilege such as attorney–client relationships. CNN found itself in contempt of a court order when it ran excerpts of taped conversation between Manuel Noriega and his lawyer; the tapes were given to CNN by a third party. CNN was found guilty of violating the confidentiality of a legal relationship (Day, 2000).

Whether actions by third parties such as the wife's lawsuit or stealing tapes of privileged conversations become more common remains to be seen, but it is wise for journalists to factor third parties into their decision making.

Confidentiality and Third Parties

Withholding information doesn't always take the form of journalists withholding publication of a photograph or video or some piece of information. When journalists promise sources confidentiality, it becomes their duty to withhold information from third parties under certain circumstances.

Third parties such as law enforcement officials seeking information, attorneys preparing a defense or prosecution, or even the courts can become involved in the journalist–source relationship.

> *It is still far from clear whether journalists must protect their sources or are obligated to share information.*

Similar to the medical, legal, and religious professionals' relationships with clients, journalists have a duty to protect their sources. This is recognized by shield laws in some states. Since the Cohen versus Cowles (1991) decision allowed sources to sue for breach of confidentiality, the media have become more careful in granting anonymity. However, it is still far from clear whether journalists must protect their sources or are obligated to share information; many a journalist has spent time in jail for refusing to do so. To them, the ethical choice was clear, but the legal system saw it differently.

In these cases, using a framework for making ethical decisions after the fact is less important than considering the possibility of third parties before taking action. It may not change the decision, but at least journalists will be prepared for the role third parties may play.

In one unusual case, a reporter's spouse inadvertently became a third party to a confidentiality dispute (Duhe, 2002). The TV reporter asked her husband to drive her to the home of a confidential source as a safety measure. Unable to get information about the source from the reporter, prosecutors tried to circumvent the confidentiality arrangement by having the husband subpoenaed to testify before a grand jury.

Although such an occurrence is rare so far, it is nevertheless instructive for journalists to consider in advance the possible consequences to third parties who do not have the same First Amendment rights as reporters.

When Third Parties Seek Publicity

Besides having information such as the name of a source that third parties sometimes want, outsiders may get involved because the media has something else they want: publicity. At other times, third parties' concern may be genuine, but their involvement causes problems.

After a school shooting in Stockton, California, the media relations officer found himself dealing not only with families and the media, but also with third parties such as a politicians and pop stars (Briggs, 1990). At a memorial service, staffers of the governor attempted to control the event and the media's questioning of the governor's stance on gun control.

Shortly after the service, a well-intentioned Michael Jackson sought to visit children still recovering at a local hospital. A feeding frenzy of fans ensued.

From that experience, the press officer offered advice that journalists as well as public relations practitioners can benefit from: Think long and hard about third parties, and expect the unexpected, preparing for potentially serious complications.

The issue of how concerned a physician should be with third party harms and broader social concerns is increasingly prominent throughout the healthcare system. This issue can most clearly be seen in the context of financial concerns where the high cost of providing health care often taxes resources available for others—both other patients, and society at large (through lost opportunity costs when healthcare uses resources that might be devoted to other issues and programs). Managed care organizations have attempted to incorporate this context into the physician–patient relationship by organizing insurance schemes around "group costs" and premiums that are supposed to reflect resource conservation. In this, doctors have been encouraged to consider the costs of treatment alternatives, and to make decisions based not only on effectiveness, but on cost. Thus, a less expensive medication that may be slightly less effective but still achieve treatment goals, or which has more side effects but not side effects that pose significant dangers, might be recommended over more costly medications.

The reactions of both the public and the medical profession itself, however, have been extremely negative toward this idea. Although it is widely recognized that health care costs are one of the most important crises facing the United States, it is perhaps even more widely believed that addressing these costs should not be done through intrusion on the doctor–patient relationship. As a society (and, for doctors, as a profession), it is accepted as a fundamental truth that treatment decisions should be based on factors related to "benefit to the patient in question" (May, 2002) rather than broader social concerns. Although, as we have seen, there are exceptions to this, where significant and imminent harms are posed to third parties, the strong presumption must remain that an obligation of confidentiality to the patient must take precedence over the social goods a physician might hope to achieve through breaking confidentiality.

Conclusion

People in society are interdependent beings; what affects one affects another, like dominos. In journalism, stakeholders are usually defined at the primary level. Seldom does one consider other layers of stakeholders; the third parties such as families, children, and even people unlucky enough to be in the wrong place at the wrong time. This article has argued the need for a broader definition of stakeholders in ethical dilemmas to include third parties in ethical considerations. Journalists should expand their thinking to include consideration of others. As always, they should consider a range of options available for doing their duty to inform the public while also minimizing harm to third parties.

Journalists can also benefit by expanding their thinking to compare themselves with other professions that have similar roles in society. Here we have compared anthropologists work to journalists, and contrasted the arrangement these professionals have regarding confidentiality and disclosure.

With regard to physicians, we have suggested expansion of the Tarasoff (1976) principle to a broader context, one that would encourage more disclosure in certain circumstances.

The broader lesson we can take away from these more focused issues is the value of applying different views, theoretical frameworks, and starting points to the ethical issues in any profession. An interdisciplinary perspective is an approach can shed new light on well-worn professional problems.

Note

1. To the extent that resources gained through celebrity attention are unfair, the argument that confidentiality should be violated because of the good that could come from raising public awareness in this way would collapse.

References

AMA principles of medical ethics. (2001). Retrieved September 7, 2004, from http://www.cirp/library/statement/ama

Anonymous. (1994). Court allows suit by spouse not in article. *Media & the Law, 18*(3), 7–8.

Bok, S. (1989). *Lying: Moral choice in public and private life.* New York: Vintage.

Borden, S. (1996). Choice processes in a newspaper ethics case. *Communication Monographs, 64,* 65–81.

Briggs, W. (1990). Intercepting interlopers: The public relations implications of handling third parties at the scene of a disaster. *Public Relations Journal, 46*(2), 40–41.

Cohen v. Cowles, 501 U.S. 663 (1991).

Day, L. (2000). *Ethics in media communications: Cases and controversies* (3rd ed.). Belmont, CA: Wadsworth.

Duhe, S. (2002). The spouse is squeezed: A South Carolina TV reporter's attempt to conceal her source. In P. Patterson & L. Wilkins (Eds.), *Media ethics: Issues and cases* (4th ed., pp. 36–38). Boston: McGraw-Hill.

Feinberg, J. (1984). *Harm to others.* New York: Oxford University Press.

Fulgham, K. (2004). A letter to help children cope. Retrieved May 19, 2004, from http://www.journeyofhearts.org/jofh/grief/fulgham

Grimes, T., & Drechsel, R. (1996). Word-picture juxtaposition, schemata, and defamation in television news. *Journalism & Mass Communication Quarterly, 73*(1), 169–180.

Lambeth, E. (2000). Two steps forward, one more to go? *Journal of Mass Media Ethics, 15,* 273–275.

Larson, M. (1977). *The rise of professionalism.* Berkeley: University of California Press.

May, T. (2002). *Bioethics in a liberal society: the political framework of bioethics decision making.* Baltimore: Johns Hopkins University Press.

Mill, J. (1956) *On liberty.* Indianapolis, IN: Bobbs Merrill. (Original work published 1859)

Rawls, J. (1971). *A theory of justice.* Cambridge, MA: Harvard University Press.

Smith-Fullerton, R. (2002, August 7–12). *Covering kids: Are journalists guilty of exploiting children?* Paper presented at Media Ethics Division, AEJMC conference, Miami Beach, FL.

Sontag, S. (1977). *On photography.* New York: Anchor.

Tarasoff v. Regents of the University of California, 551 P 2d 334 (Cal 1976).

Journal of Mass Media Ethics, *19*(3&4), 293–306
Copyright © 2004, Lawrence Erlbaum Associates, Inc.

Cases and Commentaries

The *Journal of Mass Media Ethics* publishes case studies in which scholars and media professionals outline how they would address a particular ethical problem. Some cases are hypothetical, but most are from actual experience in newsrooms, corporations, and other agencies. We invite readers to call our attention to current cases and issues. (A special need exists for good cases in advertising and public relations.) We also seek names of both professionals and academicians who might write commentaries.

I wrote the following case based on David Shaw's analysis of the *Los Angeles Times'* relationship to the Staples Center. Shaw is the *Times'* media reporter.

Louis W. Hodges, Editor
Knight Professor of Ethics in Journalism, Emeritus
Washington and Lee University
Lexington, VA 24450
540–463–8785

Tearing Down the Walls

As this issue of the *Journal of Mass Media Ethics* demonstrates, many ethics issues dog a variety of professions. Conflicts of interest, for example, are to be found in the practice of law, medicine, engineering, and journalism.

One common internal conflict that has long plagued journalism is that between the newsroom and the counting house—editorial and business sides. The long-standing tradition in the mainline press has been creation of a thick wall separating those who run the business of the newspaper from those who produce the news. Almost universally, the moral standard is to maintain fierce editorial independence from the business office—to prevent business concerns from influencing editorial decisions.

Business management at the *Los Angles Times* proved the strength of the standard when it entered a profit-sharing agreement with a new downtown sports and entertainment arena, the Staples Center. On October 10, 1999, the *Times* published a special issue of its Sunday magazine devoted entirely to the new Staples Center. Most of the paper's journalists learned only then that executives at the *Times* had arranged a profit split from the magazine between the *Times* and the Center. More than 300 reporters and editors signed a petition that demanded an apology and thorough review by their publisher, Kathryn Downing.

She did apologize. Responding to the journalists' protest, Mark Willes, chairman and CEO of the *Times'* parent company, Times Mirror, admitted "that the profit-sharing agreement had been a mistake."

According to David Shaw (1999; Pulitzer-winning media reporter at the *Times*), when Willes took over management of the *Times*, he thought he had to do something drastic to improve the company's standing on Wall Street. One part of his plan was to dismantle "The Wall between the editorial and business departments … ." Staples was one result.

On the business side, Shaw (1999) wrote that many people in advertising did not grasp "why the Staples profit-sharing arrangement was a mistake. They think the paper didn't do anything wrong. They don't understand what all the fuss is about." Willes reflected the position of management: "(H)e was convinced that greater interdepartmental cooperation—and a more focused, aggressive approach to promoting and selling advertising for the paper—would bring in new revenues … ," clearly a worthy goal.

On the journalism side, ethical standards and practice were reaffirmed in a letter to the newsroom by Otis Chandler, *Times* publisher for 20 years and a heroic figure in American journalism. Chandler's letter was a stinging rebuke of *Times* business management for "unbelievably stupid and unprofessional handling of the Staples special section … . If a newspaper … loses credibility with its community … [it is] the most serious circumstance I can possibly envision … . Respect and credibility for a newspaper is [sic] irreplaceable."

Ethicists Stephen Klaidman and Tom Beauchamp (1987), in *The Virtuous Journalist*, provided a stark rendering of the conflict between newsroom and counting room:

> Although business executives of news organizations should be as concerned about profits as those who sell cars or soap, journalists should be indifferent to whether their daily work—reporting or editing—directly enhances profitability or otherwise affects an employer's interests. (p. 217)

References

Klaidman, S. & Beauchamp, T. L. (1987). *The virtuous journalist*. New York: Oxford.
Shaw, D. (1999, December 20). Special report: Crossing the line. *L. A. Times*.

Commentary 1
"So What's the Big Deal?"
The General Unimportance of Ethics

Calpurnia, Caesar's wife, set the standard. Not only must the Virtuous Journalist do his workaday job—get the truth, write the truth, and publish without fear or favor—he must go much, much, farther. He must not participate in a publishing project with partners who might be expected to have strong opinions on the subject of the project; he must not be seen to be on the same staff with people who collaborate with persons with strong opinions; he must not allow the slightest perception to arise in this or in any hypothetical community that by any set of associations he might ever, at some future date, be on the same planet with people reasonably suspected of ... . But possibly I overstate.

I will argue that *Times* reporters' and editors' indignation is understandable, but misplaced. My argument is relatively straightforward: First, there was no corruption, no reprehensible influence on the paper's news and editorial function; and second, this kind of promotion is not unusual, and as a matter of fact, its name is legion, and it has useful social purposes, including the purpose of making money; and third, given the scarcity of newspapers in the nation that make the least pretense of integrity, it is unwise to discourage innovative thinking about the bottom line in the ones we have. We want them around for a long time.

Let's take these points one at a time.

1. "Corruption" in its original meaning is decomposition, breaking up, as of a body after death, the destruction of the unity and integrity of bodily systems by small things that eat it away and cause its parts to separate, to lose their meaning, so that they become something foul, unclean. Most especially it applies to that degree of decomposition that occurs before the body swells and bursts, when it outwardly appears the same as it always was, but internally it has been totally changed, subjected to masters unheard of in life, rearranged for purposes other than its own. Corruption in journalism means, then, in very brief, purchased advocacy in the guise of honestly discovered and objectively reported truth. The newspaper looks the way it always looked, sounds the way it always sounded, but it is subject to new masters, and its tendency is no longer its own, but theirs. A corrupt newspaper is the dead body of a newspaper; a corrupt journalist is (internally) the corpse of a journalist.

Did this happen to the *LA Times*? Nonsense. The very fact that 300 reporters and editors were unaware of the arrangement ruled out the possibility that their work might have been slanted by it. Had they known (try a thought experiment), and had they approved of the effort to improve the finances, how might their reporting and editing have changed? At least a favorable editorial, maybe removal of crime news from the area of the arena from the front page, maybe a general toning down of all such reporting. But none of this could happen, could it? Because no one knew, or at least, those who knew did not decide to change things. So there was no "corruption," spoiling, damage to the integrity of the product, for no person at the *Los Angeles Times* had any part in this little Sunday Supplement promotion except the people who wrote it.

2. The people who wrote it were not at fault. This promotion happened in a Sunday Supplement, a magazine; let us assume the "magazine section" that normally accompanies the Sunday paper. It is not unusual for newspapers to open their Sunday issues to promotions of almost any kind: new shopping malls, upcoming PGA opens, styles, houses, vacations, even, sometimes, education. One of the purposes of these supplements is to provide special information on the topic to those most interested in it; a second is to attract new customers to the paper by dedicating a section to their special interests; and a third is to raise money for the newspaper from the ads placed by interested parties.

Making money is good. As with any enterprise with costs, such as the salaries of the reporters and editors, the paper has to make money. It makes it through advertising: It can sell its pages for your publicity, if you're inclined to buy. That's all it has to sell, really, and it has to sell it, no newspaper will survive long on subscriptions or newsstand sales. In between advertising (Buy From Bergdorf Goodman, enticements to enrich particular merchants) and local news (Consortium Announces New Mall, alerting citizens to new developments in their community), there is the local promotion, the description of new community facilities that will simultaneously serve the public and benefit from the public's support. That ground seems to have been occupied by the Staples Center publication.

Whatever it was, it was not a straightforward ad for socks, nor a straightforward news item; it was a cooperative, collaborative, community venture, in which the *LA Times* was involved in many ways. A city newspaper, after all, is one of the first citizens of the city—it does not have to be a booster in all aspects (shouldn't be, in fact), but its interests are thoroughly intertwined with those of all the citizens, especially in their public perceptions and acts. It need make no apologies for full interested (I use that word in several senses, advisedly) participation in the city's projects.

3. Money is the root of all good, when it comes to making it possible for a newspaper to play its assigned and accepted role as informer of the public life of the community. How shall it obtain the funding it needs? In Jefferson's day, private funding (usually from the publisher) was sufficient; newsstand sales are good, subscriptions are better, but as previously mentioned, ads are necessary. If you can't sell advertising space, it will surely occur to someone to put the newspaper's news and editorial sections up for sale to the highest bidder. If we don't want to do that, and we really don't want to do that, then we have to start thinking innovatively about how to raise money in ways that do not impact the editorial integrity of the paper. These large-scale joint ventures are one possibility: Marry the newspaper's established ability to distribute information to the public purposes inherent in arenas, stadiums, parks, celebrations, and other events, to make them as effective (and well-supported) as possible. Final benefit:

Once those pages are open to support the project, they are equally open to criticize it—from complaints about the automatic rainproof roof to suggestions that the area might be better used for public housing. Having stepped into those waters, by joining in the promotional or informational effort, the paper is bound to include the entire debate, and the public interest is served.

In short, reporters and editors finding out about this effort after it was long over were whimpering before they were hurt. Whimpering can, of course, yield good—if the result brings up the whole question of the uses of the free press, and its place, and the means of its support, in a free society.

By Lisa H. Newton
Director, Applied Ethics Program
Fairfield University

Commentary 2
Willes Ran Into the Reality
That Journalism Is Different

There are several mantras in modern business, repeated and repeated by the gurus at business schools and the authors of books on how to improve your company: "Increase profit," "improve share value," and "enhance revenue." Some of the books and the professors offer advice on how to do that. Among the phrases used by these "ministers of motivation" are the concepts of "total quality management" and "synergy." These high priests of profit talk about creating "teams" among workers and finding "natural" relationships within businesses, among distributors and along the supply routes. If a business follows these "commandments" then "enlightenment," that is, more profit, will follow. The religious and spiritual references are, of course, intentional. If you have ever been to a seminar devoted to the issues, you understand they are believed religiously.

It is not a surprise then, that a CEO like Mark Willes would want to apply these tenets of faith to the Los Angeles Times company. It makes sense: Get departments to work together and use all their talents to improve the profitability of the company. That he, and those on the business side of the paper, would think this logical is predictable. They have read the gurus and the think tank papers, the business trade journals and books. Why not apply what works in other companies to a newspaper business? Willes ran into the reality that journalism, indeed, is different.

Example: A reporter was interviewing a well-known Harvard researcher who had released a study on the effects of refined sugar on human metabolism. The study said such commercial sugar was not a problem in the diets of people. The scientist was asked, "Who funded this research?" The answer was the refined sugar industry. So, the reporter asked, "How can people trust a study funded by the industry that benefits from its results?" The scientist became red-faced and angry, furious that his credibility had been called into question. He could not understand how anyone could possibly question his work and his honesty. But even a casual observer can see the problem. The researcher may be highly skilled with a long history of solid work. He may have won prizes in his field and been published in peer-reviewed journals. But when his funding source is the very industry he argues is guilt free, it is obvious that most people would at least question the results. There is a conflict of interest. Would the study have been released if it had found clear problems in weight gain and other health issues? Perhaps, but most people would think it unlikely. Now, imagine the resulting story if the journalist was also in the employ of the sugar industry. Would "truth" spring forth?

This is the problem faced by the Los Angeles Times Company. Managers agreeing to split profits with the source of their special edition invited questioning of their creditability. Even if some stories in the magazine had been negative toward Staples, the questions would have remained in the minds of readers aware of the deal. How can you trust the findings of someone who has a clear interest in the result?

If a company manufactures bolts and sells them to other companies, the bolts are expected to do what is promised. If they do not perform, sales will dwindle. If you are putting the bolts in your product, and you want your business to thrive, the bolts must work properly. If they do not hold well, you will find another bolt maker.

The same concept is true of journalism, but in a less tangible and, for society, much more important way. Journalism's product is news. Unlike bolts, it is to be expected that all news will be flawed in some ways. Journalists are trying to offer a summary of events, not to replay them. In the process of summarizing, reporters and editors make choices every day: How to "play" a story? What is the lead and what information is less important? Too whom? Which quotes to use or omit? Which pictures to publish on the front page in color and which to put inside in black and white? Which crowd estimate is most reliable? What context to offer?

This process makes journalism a messy business. On any given story, sources and the public will disagree on each of these issues, and more. This makes the creditability of journalists even more essential than that of most businesses. Mistakes, sloppiness, and poor choices all can erode the confidence of the people in journalists' honesty and their confidence in what journalists do. Clear conflicts of interest, or even the perception of conflicts, undermine the trust the public must have for journalists to remain credible. Why would consumers continue to buy news they can't trust to be accurate? If the news cannot be trusted, a news outlet's livelihood is at stake.

The journalist's most essential asset is creditability. It is the seed corn for our future. If we eat the seed corn, through unethical practices or conflicts of interest, the unique nature of the journalism business model breaks down. Said a different way, when publishers try to enhance profit at the expense of ethical journalism, they put the very foundation of their business at risk.

There used to be a rule in a chain of broadcast stations. It said no salesperson could enter the newsroom. Period. There was a clear wall between what the journalists were trying to do and what the sales department was trying to sell. That wall was breached in the *Los Angeles Times*—Staples Center supplement.

Perhaps the most important issue for journalists, and for citizens who understand the role of the press in a democracy, is that the United States system, as codified by the founders in the First Amendment, relies on independent, accurate information about what government is doing. That is also true of what private interests are doing, if it affects the common good. The Fourth Estate must provide that information. If its trust is constantly eroded, the public does not know whom to trust. And that can lead to dissolution of the way of life we hold dear.

By Jerry Dunklee
Professor of Journalism
Southern Connecticut State University

Commentary 3
Once Impregnable, the Walls Are Crumbling

It is a wonder, when you consider the crumbling walls between the newsroom and the business side on American newspapers in the last 25 years, that there have not been more scandals of the magnitude of the one in Los Angeles.

Once, the walls seemed impregnable. Jim Squires (1993), former editor of the *Chicago Tribune,* told how there was a time when you couldn't get from the *Trib's* business departments to its newsroom by elevator. Col. Robert R. McCormick, the owner, designed the building that way. The Colonel himself might intrude in the newsroom, but certainly no lesser mortal.

The *Trib* was not unique. When I joined the staff of *The News and Observer,* in Raleigh, NC, in 1959, the building was only a few years old and it, too, had been especially designed. The building was built with three floors, one for each of the three Daniels brothers who ran the paper. And the top floor, the least accessible one, went to brother Jonathan, who was the editor, and to his newsroom. No one from the other floors went to Jonathan's without his permission.

In most newspapers, however, it was not the design of the building, but the management structure, that underpinned the integrity of the newsroom. In 1972, when I became Executive Editor of *The Philadelphia Inquirer,* which was owned by Knight Newspapers, Inc. (later Knight-Ridder, Inc.), there were no resident publishers in the chain outside corporate headquarters. The highest ranking business executive at each paper was the General Manager, and he and the Executive Editor each reported separately to corporate headquarters in Miami through distinctly different channels. The two jointly negotiated the newsroom budget, but otherwise each was in charge of his own domain.

In Philadelphia, one of the paper's largest advertisers strolled into the newsroom one day, when building security was less rigid at metropolitan newspapers. He said he had learned that we had written an investigative story on a close friend and that he was going to cancel a million dollars in advertising if the story was not killed. I did not have to check with anyone before telling the advertiser that the story would not, repeat NOT, be killed. As for canceling the advertising, that was between him and the ad department, as I had no connection with advertising. I walked with him to the elevator and gave him directions to the advertising department. The directions apparently were good. The next day his advertising disappeared from the paper and didn't return for six months.

I never received even the mildest complaint from those on the business side. They understood that allowing advertising to dictate news content could destroy the reputation of the newspaper and shake the confidence of its readers.

The separation of editors from the business side did not endure on most papers. In the late 1970s and throughout the 1980s, newspaper ownership grew steadily more concentrated. As chains got bigger, they streamlined management and set the stage for the steadily increasing profits Wall Street was demanding from burgeoning media corporations. By the late 1980s, resident publishers had been installed at all Knight-Ridder newspapers, and editors now reported to the publishers. Newspaper corporations wanted profits to go up each year and gave publishers the authority to make this happen.

At first, not much changed. The old culture of newsroom separatism did not disappear overnight. But as the years passed, there was a tendency by publishers to draw editors ever more deeply into the business "team." Today it is common for editors to be a part of the publisher's operating committee, the group that has the responsibility for ensuring that the publisher meets the profit goals assigned to him by corporate headquarters.

The editor usually is not ex-officio or otherwise separate; he is just another committee member along with the directors of advertising, circulation, production, finance, and other assorted departments. The tone and the agenda for the meetings (usually weekly or bi-weekly) are usually set by the publisher, and it is his philosophy that mostly prevails.

The publisher, of course, may draw ethical lines differently from those commonly recognized in newsrooms. It is interesting, shocking even, to remember that after the Staples furor in Los Angeles, *Editor & Publisher* magazine polled a cross section of publishers, and a substantial majority said they would have entered into the Staples deal just as did the *Los Angeles Times*.

It is not unheard of at operating committee meetings for business department directors to challenge newsroom policies and practices, or for the advertising director to ask for the editor's help in increasing advertising linage. Sometimes, newsroom cooperation with the advertising department is put in writing and included in the goals an editor must achieve to get the maximum annual bonus.

In an article for the *American Journalism Review*, Geneva Overholzer (1998) quoted from one Knight-Ridder editor's bonus goals:

> Communication with Advertising and Production—7 points
>   A. To help [the paper] achieve its goal of increasing advertising revenue through shifts from competitors' share of the market, we will foster a relationship with the advertising division that results in a constant exchange of information on matters of mutual concern. These include special sections produced by the newsroom that might result in additional advertising; the opportunity to sell adjacent to regular news features; and flexibility on our part, when appropriate, on the placement of advertising on pages with news content. (p. 187)

It is easy, of course, for a courageous editor to forgo a handful of bonus points and a small percentage of income to stand on principle. It is more difficult when the resources of the newsroom are at stake. From attending operating committee meetings and from ongoing discussions with the business side, the editor is conditioned to realize that the publisher might very well lose his job if profits fail to rise—even if the paper is already showing a profit of 20% or more, which is two or three times what the average Fortune 500 corporation makes. Thus, the editor knows that lagging profit margins almost certainly will cause the publisher to make budget cuts.

Will helping the advertising director sell more advertising stave off cuts in news hole and newsroom staff or prevent layoffs? What if the editor knows staff and news hole are already so thin that the paper is not adequately serving its readers? Where is the ethical line? Were there good reasons for the walls between journalism and business? What does an editor do to avoid being co-opted through constant exposure to business pressures? It is easy to drift slowly into major compromises.

One approach is for editors to constantly mull over—and debate internally—the blurring ethical lines and to work out for themselves the issues on which the lines should never be indistinct. This means attending seminars on ethics, reading articles, and sharpening one's antennae well in advance of an actual problem. This way, an editor can define the lines of battle rather than simply drift into a bad decision.

By Eugene L. Roberts
Professor of Journalism
University of Maryland

References

Overholzer, G. (1998, December). "Editor, Inc." *American Journalism Review.*
Squires, J. (1993). *Read all about it: The corporate takeover of America's newspapers.* New York: Random House.

Commentary 4
Ethical Principles: Integration or Separation?

American and world societies are slow to believe and accept that ethically and pragmatically integration is usually, but not always, a superior principle to separation. American society has come to accept this notion in regard to some issues (such as Black–White education and marriages), but still remains unenlightened as to this principle's application to other areas of living.

A "wall of separation" philosophy is almost always an anti-ethical edict, in my opinion. Yet we still hear it constantly. There should be a wall of separation between: the church and the government; home life and work life; the editorial and business sides of journalism; *ad nauseam*. Get real. It is increasingly impossible to separate the two. Quit trying, and accept that what often appear to be polar-opposite events are frequently and inevitably linked and interdependent co-determinants.

Instead of arguing about separation, we should focus on global ethics, moral maxims and propriety principles such as: (a) human worth and dignity; (b) transparency; (c) accountability; and (d) servanthood.

The mass media industry today is big business; newspapers, magazines, radio, TV, and cable broadcasters are normally part of larger commercial conglomerates. The key is to have both or all sides operate using ethical principles, rather than believing that one role or another needs to be a watchdog over the other. Public transparency and ultimate accountability, if practiced, will normally assure ethical endeavors. Internal human conscience and external societal laws guide appropriate behavior for most, but not all, individuals.

In the particular case of the *Los Angeles Times* having a profit-sharing agreement with the Staples Center, get over it. That's the way the world works today. Fast food restaurants are on college campuses. Businesses in industrialized nations routinely outsource labor to third-world countries. Churches play bingo, states run lotteries, governments pork barrel projects. As long as such activities do not violate human respect and dignity and contribute to society as a whole (servanthood), and so long as transparency and accountability are satisfied, integration is normally both a preferable philosophy and a preferential practice to separation.

Please do not interpret these comments to mean that the author is a situationalist and that I believe anything is relative, contingent to, and/or dependent upon everything else. Nothing could be farther from the truth. I have just found that often seemingly polar viewpoints can frequently both be at least partially correct. We do not have to choose between unity/diversity, art/science, equality/affirmative action, freedom/responsibility, teaching/research, short-range/long-term, micro/macro, private/public, ethics/profits, technology/human resources, or even integration versus separation. Both perspectives are important and need to be blended into creative solutions to complex problems. Nonetheless, integration is the stronger ethical principle and should dominate, but not totally replace, separation as a theme and template for human behavior.

By Andrew Sikula, Sr.
Richard G. Miller Distinguished Professor of Management
Lewis College of Business

Commentary 5
It's Not Journalists Who Would Tear Down the Wall

You hire an architect to renovate your house. A wall stands in the way of his plans, so he hires a construction worker to tear it down. When the carpenter rips through the sheet rock, the roof caves in: Neither knew it was a load-bearing wall.

The architect is Mark Willes. The house is the *Los Angeles Times*. The wall separates the editorial and business divisions of a newspaper. Willes peddled breakfast cereal for General Mills so well that Times-Mirror, worried about sagging profits and its image on Wall Street, hired him in 1995 as its chief executive officer. He decreed that he would blow up—with "a ba-zooka, if necessary"—the wall between the editorial side and the business side.

He hired as publisher Kathryn Downing, a corporate lawyer from the company's legal publishing division. Between them, they have precisely zero days' experience of working in daily journalism. They may have taken courses in business ethics and legal ethics, but never an ethics class explaining the vastly different role of journalism.

Is it any wonder the house caved in?

Willes and Downing saw their task as making the company more profit-able. There is no question that Willes and Downing—booted from the *Times* in the wake of the Staples fiasco—are smart people who did what they thought was right.

Therein lies the problem: They had no experience in journalism, which, when done right, can conflict with the business goal of maximizing profits. Staples-like ethical lapses are bound to occur when people without report-ing or editing experience call the shots.

Please do not read this and think I believe that newspapers should be loss-leaders for their owners. My 401k enjoys stock granted by my news-paper chain. I root for the hometown teams for no other reason than know-ing that victories sell more newspapers than losses. And I know from expe-rience that newspapers can be more fearless when they operate from financial strength—or at least hire higher-paid lawyers.

As a midlevel editor for the business section of a newspaper that is part of a publicly traded company, I see trouble from three directions:

1. Journalists who do not understand, at least in theory, the need for newspapers to make money by delivering an audience for advertisers.

In more than 15 years in daily journalism, I have sat near reporters and editors who assume growth and business are inherently evil. (These usu-ally are the same people who cannot balance a checkbook, cannot compute a percent-change, and cannot understand why a 15-part series on the taxa-tion of tsetse flies in Tegucigalpa likely will not attract readers of a South-ern U.S. newspaper.)

Good journalists should understand the pressures on the business side, even as they make decisions that can put more pressure on the business side. Journalists should not pander to advertisers or readers by writing sto-ries only about topics guaranteed to interest upscale readers who are the chief demographic focus of advertisers. Instead, journalists should pro-duce lively newspapers that will make advertisers want to buy access to their ever-growing audience.

On one hand, journalists should show a degree of sensitivity to advertis-ers. (Example: I've made sure stories about a bank robbery did not run next to bank ads. But I made sure the bank robbery story ran elsewhere in that paper.)

On the other hand, journalists should report without fear or favor. Among the lesser reasons, aggressive reporting builds the credibility that the business side uses as a key selling point of newspapers.

As editors told me when I was a reporter, I now tell my reporters in a metaphor-mixing way: Feel free to bite the hand that feeds you, but you better hit the bulls-eye. Translation: Reporters know that stories critical of advertisers will receive special attention from higher-ups. You can write them, but make sure you are right.

2. Marginal products that make money but ultimately cheapen the newspaper's reputation.

I opened up a recent "Autos" section of my paper and there it was—a 36-point headline that included an "it's" that should have been an "its." Granted, the news side prints more than its share of grammatical mistakes, but not nearly with the frequency (and large point size) of "advertorial" products that look like newsroom products but actually are created by the advertising department. The stories in those sections suggest that every auto is perfect, reasonably priced, and sold by caring dealerships that lose money on every sale but make up for it in volume.

These wolf-in-sheep's-clothing sections come with a reminder in small text that it is not an editorial product, but I bet most readers do not know the difference. In a perfect world, newspaper sections that look as if they were produced by the newsroom actually would be produced by the news-room. As it is, those "special advertising sections" suggest we'll be happy to jive readers on behalf of advertisers who pay us enough.

3. Business-side workers who do not understand the need for editorial integrity.

Notice that it is not journalists who are clamoring to tear down the wall between "church" and "state." With no exceptions I can think of, it always is the business side that seeks to sidle up to the news side in hopes of sell-ing more ads. What the business side forgets is that credibility is the goose that lays their golden eggs.

In a perfect world, advertising sales representatives would understand journalism ethics. They would know that the paper's credibility is key to what they are selling, and they can make a direct impact on a paper's credibility.

The business side should teach advertisers that they are only buying space—not access to news content. They would not try to act as intermedi-aries between the newsroom and advertisers. They would say "no" to deals with advertisers that could sully the paper's credibility. Ad reps would feel free to pitch story ideas to editors, but with no more expectation than anyone else in the community pitching a story idea. Publishers would prove to advertisers that threatening to pull advertising cannot sway the news product.

The bottom line: All ethical businesses have lines they will not cross to make more money. (As critic Michael Moore put it: "If General Motors' main responsibility is to its shareholders, why not just get out of the car business altogether and start selling crack cocaine?")

The difference is that journalism has more lines that should not be crossed. The key is having top executives with journalism experience who can see the lines.

By Chris Roberts
Sunday Business Editor
The State
Columbia, SC

Journal of Mass Media Ethics, *19*(3&4), 307–320
Copyright © 2004, Lawrence Erlbaum Associates, Inc.

Book Reviews

The book editor is always seeking energetic, thoughtful reviewers for books, software packages, films, and other materials relating to teaching and research in media ethics. You may contact the editor, as listed below, to suggest an essay topic, a book, or a reviewer.

Deni Elliott
Poynter-Jamison Chair of Media Ethics and Press Policy
Department of Journalism
University of South Florida St. Petersburg
St. Petersburg, FL 33701
Elliott@stpt.usf.edu
(727) 553-4857

Advertising and the Consumer–Citizen
A Review by Richard M. Dubiel

Spring, J. (2003). *Educating the consumer-citizen: A history of the marriage of schools, advertising, and media.* Mahwah, NJ: Lawrence Erlbaum Associates, Inc. 264 pp., $24.94 (Pbk).
Reichert, T. (2003). *The erotic history of advertising.* Amherst, NY: Prometheus. 300 pp., $24.00 (Pbk).

Educating the Consumer-Citizen is a truly interdisciplinary work and defies easy categorization. At first glance, its primary value is that of an insightful multi-tiered history of mass media and advertising, but within the context of American education, history, and popular culture. Another reading will emphasize the historical-critical dimension of the book, that is, cultural criticism solidly rooted in American history.

Educating the Consumer-Citizen has the key feature of comprehensiveness, coupled to an assiduous attention to detail. This is a book suitable for use as a text in a variety of courses. What it isn't is another rant against our materialistic culture, fueled by the evildoers in advertising.

Spring introduces the reader to the early 19th century basis of a mass-consumer society and then sharpens his focus with his definitions of two key concepts.

The first is the consumer-citizen, "a person who accepts any political situation as long as there is an abundance of consumer goods" (p. 4). This consumer is different from the 19th-century model, where saving, avoiding debt, and acting in an otherwise fiscally prudent matter were the ideal. The goal becomes a personal transformation through the buying of goods. In the ideology of consumerism, the person is what he buys, that is, consumes.

Consumerism, Spring's second key concept, is understood as "Consumerist ideology" defined by his 12 "Basic Ideas" (p. 5). With apologies to the author, the main thrust of the 12 basic ideas can be grasped by mentioning three. One is that work is a virtue, evidence of good character and personal merit, and that poverty is a matter of personal responsibility and not the result of outside forces.

A second basic idea is that the goal of society should be seemingly never-ending economic growth and "the continual production of new goods" (p. 6). As previously mentioned, social virtue herein is to consume new and better products. Advertising, it follows, is good and necessary because it provides the motivation to keeping working in the endless pursuit of new products.

A third idea is the most philosophically important, particularly with regard to ethics. The adherents of this Consumerist Ideology (all of us) are "irrational and can be manipulated in his or her purchases" (p. 6).

The Consumerist Ideology becomes a fundamental religion of sorts, in that it hold that the "consumption of products will transform one's life" (p. 6). But this is an amoral ideology. The proponents of Consumerist Ideology are not concerned with ethics beyond a perpetuation of the system. Amongst other things, it is a religion without an *eschaton*.

What follows is a thorough history of how the culture of the United States has been resolutely headed in the direction of the consumer society, with the consumer-citizen at the center. A reader could be misled to believe Spring assumes that a vast conspiracy is directing the culture towards this end. But this is not a conspiracy, rather more a Hegelian system, a force that simply is. But make no mistake concerning the orientation of the author. When the concluding sentence reads, "America's cuisine, advertising, and media are its most important contributions to world culture" (p. 208), an endorsement of the Consumerist Ideology is unlikely.

The book continues to examine aspects of American history and culture through the lens of Consumerist Ideology. The chapter titles are inviting and seldom disappoint the reader: How Consumerist Ideology impacted women is treated in the chapter "Liberation With Jell-O and Wonder Bread: Educating the New Woman"; for men, "Cowboys and Jocks: Visions of Manliness." The chapter titled "The American Way and the Manufacturing of Consent" takes a turn that makes the book very contemporary in light of current political debate in the United States. Nonetheless, the author's wry style and erudition keep the book from becoming polemical. The text is firmly planted in history.

Interesting facts related to Spring's central thesis are abundant in each chapter. For example, the Civilization Act of 1819 was an attempt to send missionaries "into Indian lands to convert tribes to Christianity, farming, and hard work" (p. 8). Schools, for all Americans, became places where students learn about hard work, exhibited a good character, eventually earning more money and the "ability to consume vast quantities of material goods" (p. 10).

Architecture was influenced by the CI when the first department store opened, whether the Bon Marche in Paris (1869) or John Wanamaker (1879). Store windows were designed to pull people into the interior spaces, the "palaces of consumption." The stores themselves became hubs of social activity; one could say that shopping became a sort of quasi-religious experience.

Educating... offers criticisms of American culture that stand alone and are not mere supplements to the works of Neil Postman, Noam Chomsky, James Twitchell, or Arthur Asa Berger, to name but a few. Add to this that the book is an enjoyable read.

Tom Reichert's *The Erotic History of Advertising* approaches consumer culture from a more appreciative perspective. The tone of Reichert's book is that of a historian who is also an insider with regard to the subject. Despite Reichert's comments regarding excesses in the use of sex in advertising, there is never a tone of outright disapproval and indeed more a tone of inquiry. Does sex sell? When and to whom? For how long?

The notable value of the book is that it maps out the history of sex in advertising over a considerable timeline: 1880 to the present. The obvious conclusion is that sexy ads are not new, providing evidence that we are not losing our moral compass, at least as far as advertising is concerned.

Although we might think that contemporary ads are pushing the limits, Reichert's examples show us that the Rockford Varnish Company presented ads in the 1930's that reveal more and were far sexier than present day MTV videos or Abercrombie & Fitch catalogs.

After reviewing sex in advertising as it was seen with cigarettes, soaps, and fragrances (and much more), the author takes the reader up to the present, through the jeans market, high fashion, alcoholic beverages as well as soft drinks, to ads involving condoms, venereal disease, and better sex videos.

Does sex sell? Well yes and no, but mostly yes. How? That's a good part of the book's substance.

Reichert's tone is, again, appreciative, not censorious regarding the consumer-citizen, or the commitment of our culture to the pursuit of material possessions. There is an element of enjoyment throughout the book. The illustrations are copious and the examples used are amongst the sexiest. Unfortunately, they are all black and white and the reader cannot get the full impact of the originals, where those were large, color magazine spreads.

The ethically inclined reader might have hoped for more comment on the use of sex in advertising from the standpoint of the denigration of women or the human form. Reichert comments on objections that have been raised and points out excesses, but is not writing a book that starts out with a fundamental distrust of the use of the erotic in advertising. One word might sum up advice regarding this work: enjoy. The book is often heavy on who did what in what advertising agency but still provides a pleasurable read for a person, student or not, interested in advertising and its social and cultural impact in the United States and beyond.

❏ *Richard M. Dubiel is Professor in the Division of Communication at the University of Wisconsin-Steven Point.*

Uneven Approach to Ethical Analysis
A Review by Lawrence Souder

Good, H. (Ed.). (2003). *Desperately seeking ethics: A guide to media conduct.* Lanham, MD: Scarecrow Press. 208 pp., $29.95 (Pbk).

Howard Good has set before himself a tall order: to capture the attention of undergraduates and provoke them to grapple with a difficult subject—media ethics. Moreover, having assessed the existing textbooks in the field as ineffective, he wanted to avoid their shortcomings: They feed their audiences one-liners from the same tired group of philosophers and then offer them a surfeit of case studies for them to debate from their various perspectives. Such is indeed the strategy of texts like Louis Day's *Ethics in Media Communication: Cases and Controversies* and Paterson and Wilkins's *Media Ethics: Issues and Cases.* Editor Good experiments with a radically different approach to teaching ethics. He has directed a bevy of academics who study and teach media ethics to select some cultural medium or document, analyze it for ethical principles, and apply the principles to a case study of media conduct.

The results are uneven at best and, taken as a whole, do not offer much encouragement to repeat the experiment. Many of Good's contributors seem cavalier about following his directions. Their cultural documents don't always seem contemporary. When they do select a relevant document, their use seems trivial, and they seem to resort to smuggling in traditional philosophical foundations after all. Even those who are more careful about selecting and using cultural documents according to Good's directives seem nevertheless to produce a result that does not substantially improve on the existing texts on communication ethics.

A case in point is Chapter 1, titled "A Teacher's Last Instruction: 'Love Each Other or Die'," where Holly Stocking selects as her cultural document the life of Morrie Schwartz as told by himself in *Morrie: In His Own Words* and by Mitch Albom in *Tuesdays with Morrie: An Old Man, a Young Man, and Life's Greatest Lesson.* From Schwartz's story Stocking purports to derive the ethical principle: Journalists can make a difference in the world by promoting humane values through their discretion over story selection. Stocking, however, seems fearful of falling victim to the same "Hallmark card sentimentality" (p. 2) she points out in Schwartz's story when she resorts to a more philosophically grounded measuring rod of the Poynter Institute's, "simply good journalism" (p. 14). Morrie Schwartz's story then becomes not a source of ethical principles but a model of a life lived ethically as validated by some external collective. Stocking's move here seems to undermine the premise of Good's book and vindicate the traditional approach to teaching media ethics.

Most of the remaining chapters repeat the performance of the first seven: Essayists either treat their selected cultural documents not as a source of ethical principles but as an object of ethical criticism and smuggle in ethical principles from the standard line of philosophers, or they trivially derive ethical principles that have already been around. Furthermore, in the process we get not instruction in ethical decision-making, but ethical prescriptions from an ideologically driven critique.

Only Good's last two essayists give us some helpful ethical decision making tools legitimately derived from contemporary cultural documents. In fact, Joseph Harry in chapter 12 and Douglas Birkhead in chapter 13 alone make Good's book worth its price.

Harry offers another popular film as his cultural document: *Natural Born Killers.* In the course of summarizing the film, Harry calls our attention to its self-referential quality, which effectively shows the connection between actual violence in the world and the creation and propagation of portrayals of violence in the media. The film audience's abhorrence of violence in the real world and its simultaneous prurient interests in violence in the media are hopelessly at odds. Such a postmodern conundrum, Harry suggests, is the very catalyst that might shock us into conceiving a new media ethics.

Birkhead, in the final chapter, dutifully derives his ethical principles from a cultural document of a sort—the journalistic life of I. F. Stone, although he can't resist also appealing to the works of Homer, Alasdar MacIntyre, and the modern Greek poet Cavafy. Birkhead reviews Stone's work as a reporter, his entrepreneurial *I. F. Stone's Weekly,* and his culminating book *Trial of Socrates,* and extracts a set of precepts for ethical journalism: fair and truthful reporting, compassion for the less powerful, freedom to speak and the duty to listen, love for public debate, and respect for personal privacy. By examining Stone's actual practice of journalism, Birkhead, like Harry before him, works with his cultural document in a self-referential way: Birkhead recounts not only Stone's ethical thinking, but his thinking about ethical thinking.

In the first eleven chapters of Good's book, the contributors seem intent on telling us what decisions about media conduct are morally correct. It's not particularly helpful, however, to tell us to just say no, as Lancioni does in Chapter 10, for example, when she proclaims, "Viewers … must impose their own ethical standards by switching channels" (p. 153). Only the last two chapters make good on the editor's promise: to show us how to explore ethical choices over media conduct. The difference between the two approaches comes down to the distinction between ethics and morals: Harry and Birkhead offer frameworks for autonomous ethical thinking; the other contributors offer partisan moralizing.

Good cannot be held wholly responsible for the uneven execution of his experiment; he does after all warn us in his preface, "The contributors interpret my simple, straightforward directions in rather baroque ways" (p. viii). He can be held to account, however, for the book's conceptualization, which seems flawed. Without "the same group of tired philosophers," whose lessons have been the conscience of serious ethical thinkers, we can fall victim to poor ethical thinking and reinventing old fallacies.

This awareness of ethical traditions is essential for developing a facility for ethical thinking, but it seems to elude all but Harry and Birkhead in *Desperately Seeking Ethics.*

❏ *Lawrence Souder is Professor of Communications at Drexel University, Department of Culture and Communications.*

Real Thinking: A Moral Checklist for the Novice
A Review by Lee Ann Peck

Bivins, T. (2004). *Mixed media: Moral distinctions in advertising, public relations, and journalism.* Mahwah, NJ: Lawrence Erlbaum Associates, Inc. 240 pp., $29.95 (Pbk).

Thomas Bivins, a professor at the University of Oregon's School of Journalism and Communication, has written a book to teach and explain ethical decision making to students studying mass communication and to professionals working in both the news media and media of persuasion—

advertising and public relations. Bivins also hopes to teach these audiences to be critical consumers of the mass media; most chapters end with exercises and case studies.

Real thinking is an important part of finding answers to moral dilemmas, Bivins explains in the book's introduction. However, he says, "And real thinking can only happen if the thinkers understand as much how to think as what to think about" (p. x). How does Bivins attempt to do this? Bivins takes readers on a somewhat confusing trek through six chapters where he explains professionalism and codes of ethics, ethical and political theories, and what telling the truth and avoiding harm entails—among other topics. Finally in Chapter 7, Bivins presents readers with a seven-step checklist to help with ethical decision making.

It is perhaps helpful to look at *Mixed Media* as readers in the intended audiences: Will mass communication students embrace this book? Will media ethics professors find it useful and incorporate the text into their courses? What value will it have for working professionals? Will all these audiences have the ability to do some "real thinking" after reading and studying *Mixed Media*?

If one reads the book from beginning to end over a short period of time—not over a semester, for instance—the book can be a bit overwhelming. So much diverse information is crowded into the first six chapters that one is left spinning from a variety of details about morals, values, obligations (which Bivins says is a main theme of the book), and principles. Then, mix in the codes, the philosophers, a bit of media history and media law, and explanations of public journalism and Michael Bayles' fiduciary model, and a reader may find that there is just too much to absorb in a short period of time. However, if the sections of each chapter are tackled slowly with someone to guide and embellish discussions, the novice moral agent could possibly begin to grasp the topics presented in the book.

Media professionals, however, may find that their occupations are generalized too much by the author, who may lose these readers in the first chapter. Many of the media lapses described by Bivins are presented as if they are common occurrences: "Do public relations practitioners act on our behalf when they use spin control to obfuscate the facts?" (p. 5); "…ask an advertising major at any leading university whether there is a definition of `taste,' that he or she would be willing to follow in creating ads for their clients, regardless of what the client wants. Guess what the answer will be?" (p. 6).

Bivins discusses "media laziness" in newsrooms, too; journalists are using "whatever method of news gathering (that) is easiest and fastest" (p. 7); he's not considering that some newsroom cultures today demand this so-called "laziness" because of budget cuts and a loss of manpower. Too much generalization about the professions might mislead students and upset professionals.

The book awkwardly switches from first person "we" to third person "they"; therefore, Bivins appears to connect himself and his readers to the media professions and at other times he chooses to distance himself. Intentional or not, this back-and-forth can be confusing for the reader. Oftentimes, the book introduces philosophers and theories with the promise of more explanation in later chapters, which can also be frustrating. Case study questions in the beginning chapters seem a bit premature—even for those who are trying to do some "real thinking." Readers need more knowledge before they can answer Bivins' questions with reflection and reasoning. It is unfortunate that readers aren't introduced to Bivins' specific guidelines for decision-making until the last chapter.

Chapter 2 introduces social responsibility via James Grunig's "Linkage Concept," which involves organization input and output and the consequences of both; therefore, Immanuel Kant is introduced and dropped because Kant does not believe in considering consequences of actions—he believes in duty! William D. Ross and his six categories of obligation are then presented in the author's own words; this section is followed by a short section on libertarianism and Adam Smith, followed by some history (the work of Henry Luce of *Time* and Robert Hutchins of the Hutchins Commission), followed by a quick discussion of the ideas of journalism educator Jay Rosen, followed by Walter Lippmann's call for an objective press. All good information—but could this book be organized better?

Chapter 3 introduces readers to Michael Bayles, author of *Professional Ethics*, and Bayles' thoughts on professional-client relationships, using the models of agency, fiduciary, and paternalism. And then there is a discussion of the codes and an introduction of all the professional organizations, such as the Society of Professional Journalists and the Public Relations Society of America. Chapter 4 presents ethical theory—which includes a lot of political theory (and, yes, political theory is usually based on ethical theory, but this is not explained—although real thinkers should pick up on this). Discussing Plato's Allegory of the Cave is always an eye-opener for students—the puppeteer is the media and the prisoners chained to the wall are media consumers.

But here is a fault. It is rare that Bivins cites the original works. If students were to read citations of the original works, now that would be real thinking. Because Bivins puts so much importance on the theories he presents, he should cite the real thing, so to speak; he relies heavily on his own and other authors' interpretations of these classic Western theories.

For instance, Bivins does a disservice to readers by calling Aristotle's theory of the mean, the "Golden Mean," which can suggest "all things in moderation." Aristotle's Doctrine of the Mean does not have anything to do with moderation. Another example: Kant's Categorical Imperative had several formulations, but this is not explained—another disservice.

Take what you will from *Mixed Media*. It is an attempt to help readers think through their decisions and to help them know what to think about. However, the author tries to cover too much, and, therefore, nothing is explained as thoroughly as it could be. Being more selective—and organized—would help; for instance, putting all the ideas from one time period in one section then presenting them chronologically would go a long way toward helping students. In its present form, students could possibly take a case and work through the seven steps that Bivins provides for a final course assignment, but for day-to-day deadline-driven decisions, Bivins' method is too time-consuming—especially for those "lazy" journalists.

❏ *Lee Anne Peck is Assistant Professor of Journalism and Mass Communications at the University of Northern Colorado.*

Ethical Challenge of Global Public Relations
A Review by James M. Haney

Sriramesh, K., & Vercic, D. (Eds.). (2003). *The global public relations handbook. Theory, research, and practice.* Mahwah, NJ: Lawrence Erlbaum Associates, Inc. 564 pp., $55.00 (Pbk).

Sriramesh and Vercic contend that the growth of democracies, the development of new international trade organizations, and the expansion of the Internet and satellite communication force us to examine public relations today as a global activity. Their new reference work, *The Global Public Relations Handbook*, provides an important roadmap for discovering the current state of the public relations profession around the world.

The book profiles the status of public relations in 18 countries on 6 continents. Though most existing works only consider the practice of public relations in the United States and a handful of European countries, this effort attempts to detail communication activities in Asia, Africa, Australia, Europe, North America, and South America.

An important dimension of the book is the attention given to state of public relations professionalism in each country. The handbook clearly demonstrates that the United States is not the only country with public relations practitioners who sometimes fail to comply with professional ethical codes. Practitioners in countries like the Netherlands (p. 226) and Singapore (p. 89) often practice situational ethics. Polish public relations practitioners have a professional code of ethics, but most continue to offer benefits to journalists to ensure that their organizations receive "nonstandard advertising" in the form of desirable messages in news articles (p. 263). Many people practicing public relations in Russia belong to international professional groups with specific ethics codes, but most Russian practitioners don't see ethics codes as practical (p. 306). Others contend it is "impossible to practice ethical public relations because nobody would pay for it" (p. 307).

The contributing authors also offer important reviews of transnational public relations by foreign governments (pp. 399–424) and corporations (pp. 478–489), nongovernmental organizations involved in international public relations (pp. 490–504), and PR agencies practicing global public relations (pp. 459–477). Sriramesh ends the book with a chapter on the need for an expansion of multiculturalism in public relations education in the United States and elsewhere (pp. 505–522). This discussion supports a central thesis of the book: Scholars and practitioners alike can no longer afford to address public relations as a domestic field in light of the many forces that are driving so many organizations to work in a global environment. Given that no country has perfected the ethical practice of public relations, one can't help but wonder how many more problems will take place as domestic violators cross international boundaries in their attempt to win over new audiences.

Overall, the book provides an excellent resource on global public relations for practitioners, students, and scholars. The public relations professional will gain important information in the same way that a well written travel guide can inform a tourist about local conditions one might encounter before taking a foreign trip. University libraries will find this volume to be a valuable addition to support both undergraduate and graduate curricula. Scholars will benefit from the book's precise descriptions of local activities and the important contexts that influence public relations around the world. The material presented provides a useful foundation for more sophisticated theory building about international public relations.

❏ *James M. Haney is an Associate Professor in the Division of Communication at the University of Wisconsin Stevens Point.*

Missing What Can't Be Measured
A Review by Muriel R. Friedman

Petersen, V. (2002). *Beyond rules in society and business.* Cheltenham, England: Edward Elgar. 416 pp. (Pbk).

Living in a legalistic society that seeks certainty in numbers, it is important for us to remember that there are other ways of looking at the world. Verner C. Petersen, Professor of Organization and Management at the Aarhus (Denmark) School of Business and founder of CREDO, the Center for Research in Ethics and Decision-making in Organizations, revisits traditional humanistic values as the best hope for organizations. His observations are highly relevant for mass media charged with looking behind the assumptions guiding contemporary society.

Petersen exposes the pretenses and distortions within rationalized organizations. Although he understands the desire of management for predictable outcomes, he criticizes the cult of rules as both dehumanizing and less effective than it is assumed to be. Algorithms, or "rule by a rule," are supposed to guarantee results by removing human variability from the process. One problem is that algorithms may incorporate arbitrary standards unrelated to important parameters of quality. He notes that values that can be measured, such as productivity, eclipse organizational values that are not measurable. Subtle as well as overt corruption can occur when employees' pay is based on measurable performance scores, rather than how they uphold implicit corporate ideals.

The greater problem for Petersen is that rules circumscribe responsibility to a "9 to 5," "not in my job description" mentality. He argues that much of what we know is tacit: shared, taken-for-granted, social knowledge. Children are taught our moral fabric gradually by example and narrative. Ambiguity trains us to generalize and makes us more astute. We may be following tacit morality while seeming to break rules. Alternatively, we only look moral when we blindly follow an externally imposed moral code. He prefers "an overall coherence, anchored … in the collective unconscious. There is no single overriding principle either Kantian or utilitarian, only a tacit consistency between a multitude of possible practical judgments on the surface and the deeper layers" (p. 160). He advocates vague, universal responsibility.

Petersen demands that humans be treated as the flexible, creative, reflective species we are, rather than as simple machines. Complexity and diversity add value; rules and algorithms negate the experience and wisdom that lead to good decisions. Petersen believes his approach fosters stronger, spirited leadership.

Beyond Rules in Society and Business is a wide-ranging, sensible, accessible book. Petersen uses interesting European examples, such as the old tale of Michael Kohlhaas's doomed quest for justice. Because business discourse and practices have been insinuated into virtually all aspects of modern life, the book is highly relevant to media that should be exposing the sort of shortcomings that Petersen describes.

❏ *Muriel R. Friedman, MD is a PhD Candidate in Social Theory and Criticism at the University of Montana, Missoula.*

Chicken Soup for the Cynic's Soul
A Review by Ian Marquand

Schechter, D. (2003). *Embedded: Weapons of mass deception: How the media failed to cover the war in Iraq.* Amherst, NY: Prometheus Books. 286 pp., $26.00 (Hbk).

As the title makes clear, award-winning television producer Danny Schechter doesn't think much of the military's program of embedding journalists with combat troops in Iraq. But if his new book promises a journalistic treatment of the role the "embeds" played in the American media's coverage of the Iraq war, it delivers something different. Rather than an investigative or analytical treatise, Schechter offers a kind of daily affirmation for those who never believed in the war in the first place and whose worst expectations have come true. Think "Chicken Soup for the Anti-War/Anti-Big Media/Anti-Bush Cynic's Soul."

Although the book includes a handful of articles or essays from other sources, Schechter fills most of *Embedded* with reprints of the web blogs he wrote for his on-line service, mediachannel.org, beginning in the fall of 2002. The often-lengthy blogs (there's just a hint of Hunter Thompson sans hallucinations) include information from a variety of sources, all of which bolster Schechter's premise that everything surrounding the war and its coverage was phony and contrived to cater to a symbiotic power elite in government and corporate (primarily broadcast) media.

The blogs are arranged in sections, but not necessarily in chronological order, creating an appropriately nonlinear approach to a collection of on-line material. As a result, one can open to virtually any page and find something to make the blood boil. For readers wishing to get right to the guts of Schechter's argument, go first to his introductory essay, and then skip to "A Call for Media Activism" on page 241. If those intrigue you, dive in for a feast of outrage.

❑ *Ian Marquand is the Special Projects Coordinator with KPAX-TV in Missoula, Montana.*

Speaking Out
A Review by Ian Marquand

Levinson, N. (2003). *Outspoken: Free speech stories.* Berkeley, CA: University of California Press. 372 pp. $29.95 (Hbk).

Nan Levinson easily could have titled her collection of free speech profiles "Out On A Limb," because that's where most of her subjects ended up because of their beliefs, their ethical choices, their challenges to authority, or their willingness to contradict the status quo. This is a book that may lead to spontaneous outbursts of "How dare they!" Those on the political and social left will steam over Levinson's tales of government paranoia, bureaucratic heavy-handedness, official timidity, and outright censorship. Meanwhile, those on the right may conclude that many of Levinson's subjects are unpatriotic or immoral social misfits who got just what they deserved.

Some subjects—comic artist Mike Diana's extreme "splatterzine" art, porn-star-turned-performance-artist Annie Sprinkle's "Public Cervix Announcement," or L.A. fire fighter Steve Johnson's insistence on having his "Playboys" in a mixed-gender fire house—may arouse disapproval on both sides of the fence. (Although Levinson is firmly planted on the left side of the culture war, even she is not immune from occasionally cocking an eyebrow at her subjects.)

Outspoken could become polemic; instead, it allows us to meet the human beings behind the conflicts. Each story follows a comfortable narrative formula: We meet people in their homes and offices, learn something about who they were before controversy found them, then learn in precise detail what happened to force them into taking a stand.

Levinson agilely weaves in the historical, legal, and social context in which events occurred. Although her own social commentary at times seems redundant, the writing is straightforward and descriptive, the tone intimate and compassionate, and the sources extensively footnoted. Some stories may be familiar: ex-citizen Margaret Randall's persecution by the Immigration and Naturalization Service because of her Latin American writings; New Hampshire schoolteacher Penny Culliton's dismissal over her use of gay-themed texts in high school classes; Kwame Mensah's imprisonment as an Army conscientious objector during the first Gulf War. Others will be unknown. Perhaps most significantly, each story demands that we examine our own capacity for tolerance as well as the strength of our own convictions, essentially begging the question, "Would you have had the guts to do that?"

❏ *Ian Marquand is the Special Project Coordinator with KPAX-TV in Missoula, Montana*

Books Received

Andrejevic, M. (2004). *Reality TV: The work of being watched*. Lanham, MD: Rowman & Littlefield Publishers. 253 pp., $28.95 (Pbk).
Cappo, J. (2003). *The future of advertising: New media, new clients, new consumers in the post-television age*. New York: McGraw Hill. 260 pp., $24.95 (Hbk).

Dadge, D. (2004). *Casualty of war: The Bush administration's assault on a free press.* Amherst, NY: Prometheus Books. 349 pp., $26.00 (Hbk).

Darian, S. (2003). *Understanding the language of science.* Austin: University of Texas Press. 248 pp., $27.95 (Pbk).

Dor, D. (2004). *Intifada hits the headlines: How the Israeli press misreported the outbreak of the second Palestinian uprising.* Bloomington: Indiana University Press. 185 pp., $19.95 (Hbk).

Douglas, S. (2004). *Listening in: Radio and the American imagination.* Minneapolis: University of Minnesota Press. 415 pp., $19.95 (Pbk).

Gorham, J. (Ed.). (2004). *Annual editions: Mass media 04/05.* Guilford, CT: McGraw-Hill/Dushkin. 226 pp., $20.31 (Pbk).

Hirsh, J. (2004). *After image: Film, trauma, and the holocaust.* Philadelphia: Temple University Press. 213 pp., $21.95 (Pbk).

Horton, A. (2004). *Screenwriting for a global market: Selling your scripts from Hollywood to Hong Kong.* Berkeley: University of California Press. 210 pp., $19.95 (Pbk).

Littlejohn, D. (Ed.) *Metro letters: A typeface for the Twin Cities.* Minneapolis: University of Minnesota. 160 pp., $29.95 (Pbk).

Murphy, P., & Kraidy, M. (Eds.). *Global media studies: Ethnographic perspectives.* New York: Routledge. 313 pp., $27.95 (Pbk).

Parker, R. (2003) *Free speech on trial: Communication perspectives on landmark Supreme court decisions.* Tuscaloosa: University of Alabama Press. 344 pp., $29.95 (Pbk.).

Rapping, E. (2003). *Law and justice as seen on TV.* New York: New York University Press. 309 pp., $19.00 (Pbk).

Rayner, P., Wall, P., & Kruger, S. (2004). *Media studies: The essential resource.* London: Routledge. 285 pp., $26.95 (Pbk).

Saunders, K. W. (2003). *Saving our children from the First Amendment.* New York: New York University Press. 307 pp., $48.00 (Hbk).

Soley, L. (2002). *Censorship Inc.: The corporate threat to free speech in the United States.* New York: Monthly Review Press. 308 pp., $23.95 (Pbk).

Szasz, T. (2004) *Words to the wise: A medical-philosophical dictionary.* New Brunswick, NJ: Transaction Publishers. 258 pp., $34.95 (Hbk).

Vaidhyanathan, S. (2001). *Copyrights and copywrongs: The rise of intellectual property and how it threatens creativity.* New York: New York University Press. 255 pp., $17.95 (Pbk).

Whittaker, J. (2004). *The cyberspace handbook.* London: Routledge. 321 pp., $25.95 (Pbk).

Wilson, W. C., Gutierrez, F., & Chao, L. (2003). *Racism, sexism, and the media: The rise of class communication in multicultural America.* Thousand Oaks, CA: Sage Publications. 327 pp., $39.95 (Pbk).

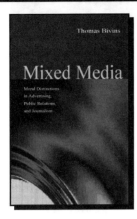

MIXED MEDIA
Moral Distinctions in Advertising, Public Relations, and Journalism
Thomas Bivins
University of Oregon

This text introduces readers to the tools necessary for making moral and ethical decisions regarding the use of mass media. The focus is on the three mass media industries most pervasive in today's society: the news media (journalism), advertising, and public relations. In his exploration of ethical issues and media, author Thomas Bivins guides students to understand not what the "right" answers are, but to identify those answers that are most appropriate within the given context. Identifying those to whom the answers are the most appropriate is a major concern of this book. Readers will come away with a greater appreciation for the complexities of making a moral decision and will develop a personal "yardstick" by which to measure their decisions.

The chapters in this text offer insights on:
* similarities and differences among the ethical dilemmas faced by the mass media;
* common ground on which to evaluate media behavior;
* media obligations;
* professional ethics;
* ethical theory and its application to the modern media; and
* considerations of truth and harm.

This text has been developed for courses covering ethics in public relations, advertising, and journalism. Offering valuable lessons applicable to all forms of communication, *Mixed Media* serves as a critical starting point for understanding and developing answers to ethical questions. These lessons serve not only to better students' ability to make ethical decisions, but also to better the media professions as they become practitioners in the mass media industry.

Contents: Introduction. What Makes an Ethical Issue? Moral Claimants, Obligation, and Social Responsibility. The Media and Professionalism. Ethical Theory. To Tell the Truth. Avoiding Harm. A Checklist for Ethical Decision Making. **Appendix:** Media Codes of Ethics.
0-8058-4257-8 [paper] / 2004 / 240pp. / $29.95
Prices are subject to change without notice.

Lawrence Erlbaum Associates, Inc.
10 Industrial Ave., Mahwah, NJ 07430–2262
201–258–2200; 1–800–926–6579; fax 201–760–3735
orders@erlbaum.com; www.erlbaum.com

35838736OO

SCREENWRITING WITH A CONSCIENCE

Ethics for Screenwriters

Marilyn Beker

Loyola Marymount University

A Volume in LEA's Communication Series

"Wise and urgent advice to young screenwriters from a committed and passionate teacher. Beker speaks with years of experience and a great generosity of spirit."

—**Atom Egoyan**
Writer/Director, *Exotica, The Sweet Hereafter, Ararat*

"This text would be appropriate for courses in fundamentals of screenwriting but also, perhaps especially, for critical studies and film theory and history courses. Given the vast public attention to this subject, I should think this could be a crossover book that appeals to audiences beyond the academy."

—**Richard Walter**
University of California at Los Angeles

Screenwriting With a Conscience: Ethics for Screenwriters is for screenwriters who care deeply about what they write; who are aware that movie images matter and can influence audiences; and who want to create meaningful screenplays that make powerful statements while entertaining and winning over audiences. A user-friendly guide to ethical screenwriting, this book makes the case that social responsibility is endemic to public art while it emphatically champions First Amendment rights and condemns censorship.

In this dynamic and practical volume, author Marilyn Beker provides methods for self-assessment of values, ideas, and ethical stances, and demonstrates the application of these values to the development of plot, character, and dialogue. Screenwriters are introduced to ethical decision making models and shown—through specific film examples—how they can be utilized in plot and character development. In addition, specific techniques and exercises are supplied to help screenwriters determine the difference between "good" and "evil," to write realistic and compelling characters based on this determination, and to present "messages" and write dialogue powerfully without preaching. This book also puts forth a livable work philosophy for dealing with the ethics of the screenwriting business, and presents a viable personal philosophy for surviving in the screenwriting world.

Screenwriting With a Conscience: Ethics for Screenwriters is a practical, dynamic guide for the ethics-conscious screenwriter. It is intended for screenwriters at the student and professional level, and is appropriate for beginning to graduate screenwriting courses in film and English programs, and for film courses dealing with Ethics in the Media.

Contents: Preface. Introduction. **Part I:** *Why? Ethics? For Screenwriters?* Message and Meaning. The Certainty of Why. Social Responsibility. What's Art Got to Do With It? **Part II:** *The Certainty of What: Anything Goes?* A Glimpse of Stocking. Something Shocking. Where Have All the Elders Gone? Conscience. **Part III:** *What Really Matters.* What It's Worth. The Good, the Bad, the Blurry. Nothing Left to Chance. **Part IV:** *White Hats, Black Hats.* White Hats, Black Hats. Good. Bad. The Villanero. Practical Writing Techniques. Angelic Acts, Dastardly Deeds. Crime and Punishment. Special Circumstances. **Part V:** *Killing the Messenger.* No Sermons. Words of Wisdom. **Part VI:** *Having Written and Writing More.* What's the Idea? All's Fair in Love, War, and Showbiz? Courage. Conclusion.

0-8058-4127-X [cloth] / 2004 / 256pp. / $69.95
0-8058-4128-8 [paper] / 2004 / 256pp. / $24.50
Prices are subject to change without notice.

Lawrence Erlbaum Associates, Inc.
10 Industrial Ave., Mahwah, NJ 07430–2262
201–258–2200; 1–800–926–6579; fax 201–760–3735
orders@erlbaum.com; www.erlbaum.com